Anderson Marsh
State Historic Park

Anderson Marsh
State Historic Park

A Walking History, Prehistory,
Flora, and Fauna Tour
of a California State Park

Second Edition
Updated and Expanded

Kathleen Scavone

Anderson Marsh
State Historic Park

A Walking History, Prehistory, Flora and Fauna Tour of a California State Park.

Second Edition. Updated and Expanded

Copyright © 2022, 1999 Kathleen Scavone
All rights reserved.

This book or any portion thereof
may not be reproduced or used in any manner whatsoever
without the express written permission of the author
except for the use of brief quotations in a book review.

Second Edition of
Anderson Marsh State Historic Park
A Walking History, Prehistory, Flora and Fauna Tour
of a California State Park.

Print Edition ISBN 978-0-9673981-2-9
Ebook Edition ISBN 978-0-9673981-3-6

Cover Photo by Kathleen Scavone, Copyright © 2022

State Park Map used with permission of the State of California - The Resources Agency, DEPARTMENT OF PARKS AND RECREATION
Inside photos Courtesy of Dr. John Parker and Winifred Minden

Book design and formatting by Leo Baquero
leo_baquero@hotmail.com - layooutadaptationdesign.com

Contents

Acknowledgements. 7
Second Edition Introduction. 11
Mahatma Gandhi's Quote 13
State Park Map. 14
Overview: Anderson Marsh State Historic Park. 15
    Location 15
    Prehistoric Discoveries 16
    Historic Elements. 19
    The Andersons 19
    The Grigsbys 20
Park Trails Overview. 21
    McVicar Trail 21
    Cache Creek Trail 22
    Anderson Flats Trail 22
    Ridge Trail. 22
    Marsh Trail 23
Cache Creek Nature Trail. 25
Ridge Trail. 43
Marsh Trail 63
Anderson Flats Trail 89
McVicar Trail. 103
Photos 111
"A Walk Through Time", Award-winning documentary
about Anderson Marsh. 119
The Making Of A State Park. 121
Anderson Marsh Chronology. 133
Bibliography. 137
About the Author. 141

Acknowledgements

I would like to thank the following people for their invaluable assistance in researching and writing this book:

My brother, David Livingstone helped shape my passion for the natural world and nurtured my interest in California history. His professional archaeological expertise and suggested bibliography were immensely appreciated. I am forever grateful for the time and effort he generously gave in the editing process. His boundless support and enthusiastic participation in hikes at Anderson Marsh will remain in my heart forever.

Fortune favors me with a remarkable husband. We lived within walking distance of the jewel that is Anderson Marsh, near Cache Creek for seven years. Tom's support was vital to every stage of my work. I am particularly grateful to my sons, Eric and Justin Montgomery for their lifelong love and understanding of computers and the natural world. Thank you, also, Ariel and Weston, my step-children, for taking hikes through the marsh with me. I am grateful to my mother, Phyllis Garrison for modeling her passion for the printed word, so that I could follow suit.

I would like to acknowledge writer and professor Greg Sarris for his valuable comments upon reading a chapter of the book when it was in its infancy.

Ranger Tom Nixon's patient and generous assistance were especially appreciated. His dedication to California State Parks is evident in his informative slide presentations, interpretive hikes with students and the general public, and the energy he expends in all manner of State Parks. I would like to thank Anderson Marsh's first ranger, Floyd Lemley for his generous input as well.

I am especially grateful for Winifred Minden and Mary Van Sistine's friendship and for sharing a part of their personal past with me. Winifred shared valued family photographs so that others could glimpse into the past. I am indebted to Ted (John Theodore) Anderson for allowing me to enjoy his childhood stories centering around Anderson Marsh.

Thank you to Kathy and Peter Windrem, and Roberta Lyons for their generous assistance when their time was at a premium. Thanks goes to Elaine Mansell for her support and enthusiasm for this project. My thanks to Claudia Vogel for her lively interpretations of life at Anderson Marsh, and her generosity in sharing her notes and newspaper clippings with me.

My special thanks to State Park's Archaeologist, Breck Parkman for his highly informative contributions and for allowing me to use his photographs. His expertise in cultural and natural resources is astounding. Breck's genuine concern and love of children, the community, and the "sacred landscape" is evident throughout all of his endeavors.

I would also like to acknowledge my mentor, Dr. Victoria Patterson. Her dedication to education is phenomenal. Victoria's Native American Studies class at Sonoma State University gave me a better understanding of other cultures and a true appreciation of their commitments and accomplishments in the face of adversity.

I would like to express my gratitude to the late Dr. Weldon, and Dee Parker. Weldon and Dee entrusted me with their collection of years worth of newspaper articles, photographs and other information about their son's important work for the book.

Thank you to all of the committed volunteers, concerned citizens, and community members who fought the fight to get Anderson Marsh designated as a State Historic Park.

Finally, I would like to express my sincere gratitude to Dr. John Parker. He was extremely generous with his resources, including his dissertation and class syllabus, and photographs, allowing me free rein to use anything I needed for the book. He spent hours of his precious time walking me through the book for some much needed fine-tuning. But more than that, the State of California has John Parker to thank for his determined efforts to preserve the cultural resources of Anderson Marsh. Due to his dedication and love, we may enjoy the esthetic and historic bounty that is Anderson Marsh State Historic Park.

This book in no way represents the definitive work on Anderson Marsh, as there remains a treasure trove of information still to be told- and discovered. I take responsibility for any mistakes in editing, and any misinterpretations of the experts remain my own.

Second Edition Introduction

The world has gone through tremendous upheaval since this book was first published in 1999, with continued global warming, a world pandemic, and its ensuing social and political strife. It's become more important than ever to spend time in nature. Connecting to nature is a necessary component to remaining hopeful and optimistic. Anderson Marsh State Historic Park remains the perfect place to reset in a natural environment.

I made some updates in the book's second edition. One change at the Park is the addition of the McVicar Trail. The trail was once called the McVicar Wildlife Sanctuary, as it was once owned by the National Audubon Society, and managed by the local branch called Redbud Audubon. This trail is a result of a Partnership Agreement between the Department of Parks and Recreation and the Anderson Marsh Interpretive Association.

Since the first edition of the book was published, more awareness of the Park's many wonders has been brought to light through a documentary produced here which I discuss in a new section of the book. The documentary, "A Walk Through Time" has garnered both the Governor's Historic Preservation Award in Sacramento in 2015, as well as an Emmy Award in the category of "Historic/Cultural-Program/Special" at the 46th annual Northern California Emmy Awards ceremony in San Francisco. The documentary is available on PBS online at: https://www.pbs.org/video/kvie-viewfinder-walk-through-time/

Both the Park and my book enhance an understanding of the Pomo people's cultural traditions and technologies, where today Indigenous descendants take the time to walk their homelands, stewarding this rich natural and historical setting. Anderson Marsh State Historic Park quietly initiates all who visit into both nature and history through its many stories.

*Nature will provide for the need of the people,
It will not provide for the greed of the people.*

— Mahatma Gandhi

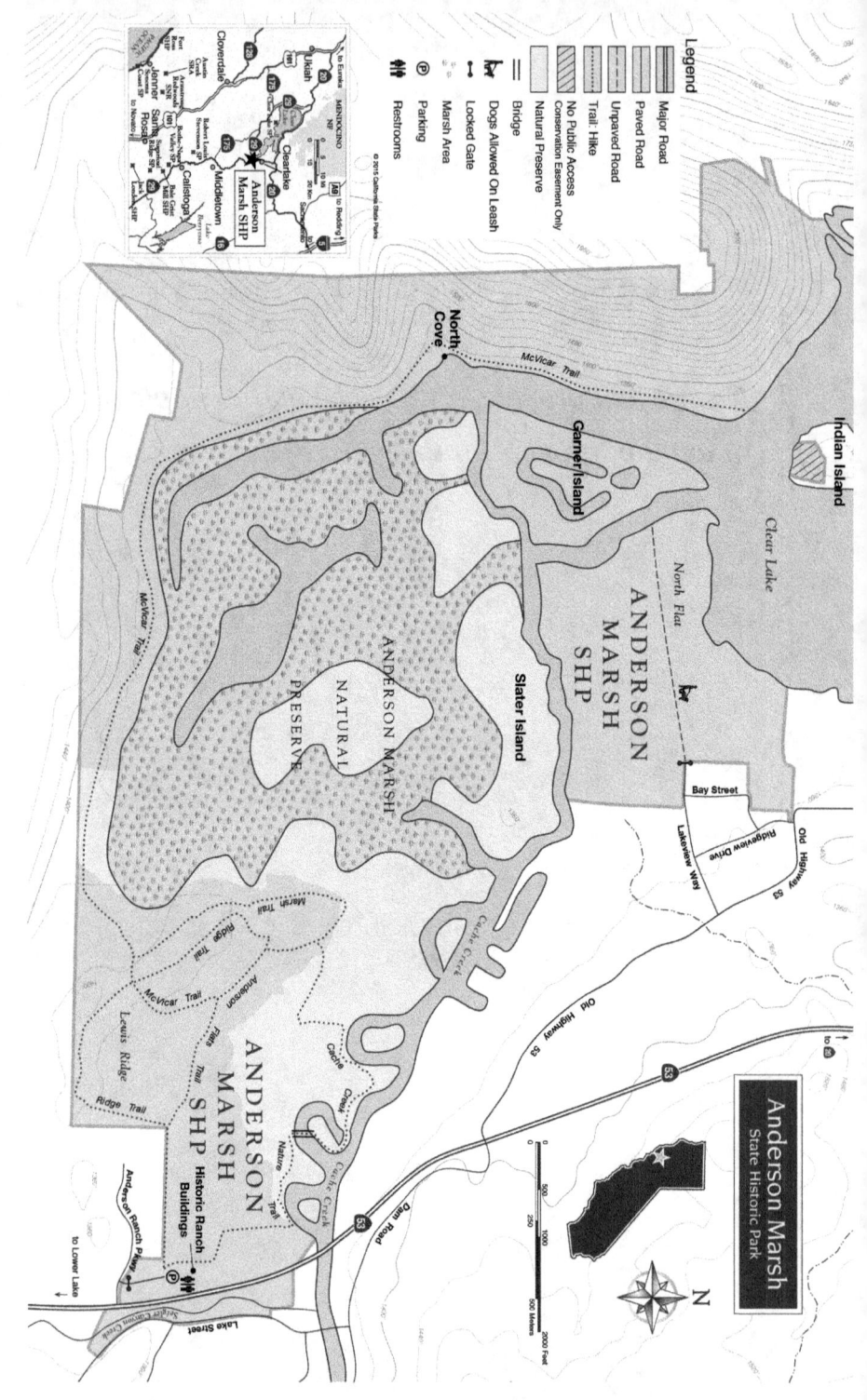

Overview: Anderson Marsh State Historic Park

Location

Anderson Marsh State Historic Park is located between the Pacific Coast and Sacramento Valley, in the Sierra Foothill and Low Coastal Mountain Landscape Province in the northern Coast Range Mountains. It is 130 miles northeast of San Francisco, and is situated at the southeast corner of Clear Lake, in Lake County on State Highway 53. Lake County is bordered on the west by Mendocino and Sonoma Counties. Colusa and Mendocino Counties border Lake County on the north, Napa and Sonoma Counties make up the southern boundary of Lake County, while to the east are Colusa and Yolo Counties. The western mountains in Lake County are the Mayacamas Mountains. Elevations in Lake County range from approximately 1,320 feet above sea level at the lake, to over 4,000 feet on local mountains such as Mt. Konocti and Cow Mountain. Temperatures in the Clear Lake basin range from 7 degrees Fahrenheit to as high as

86 degrees in winter, 55 to 91 degrees in summer, with extremes of 34 degrees and 110 degrees having been recorded. The average rainfall is 22 inches per year.

A portion of Clear Lake lies within the state park, including around 3,000 feet of its shoreline. The Clear Lake outlet channel, Cache Creek, wanders through the park, adding an additional 10,000 feet of shoreline. The creek flow has created several islands, including Slater and Garner Islands. As the state park's name implies, marshlands abound, encompassing about one-third of the park's 940 acres, as of 1991.

Prehistoric Discoveries

In 1982 the State of California acquired over 870 acres (which later swelled to 1,065 acres) in Lower Lake, California as the result of dedicated archaeologist Dr. John Parker and others who worked to preserve this beautiful slice of Lake County. In 1976, under the guidance of Sonoma State University Professor, Dr. David Frederickson, John Parker performed an intensive archaeological survey of the Anderson Marsh area. After a year of red tape and tremendous effort on Parker's part, Anderson Marsh was officially classified as an Archaeological District and listed on the National Register of Historic Places in 1977.

Laws passed in the 1970s made it mandatory to identify and protect archaeological resources in California. Environmental land use planning laws, also known under the term, "cultural resource management" have put forth requirements for firms to keep reports on prehistoric sites. These reports offer significant help in land use planning for communities.

Archaeologists studying the Clear Lake basin where Anderson Marsh State Historic Park is situated, focused on the region's Native American technology, settlement patterns, and population. Time periods for each of the criteria were determined in part by utilizing artifact typologies and obsidian hydration dating techniques. In using artifact typologies archaeologists rely on projectile point, or stone arrow tip styles that have been determined to be from distinct time periods. These then become the "indicators," or the artifacts which tell archaeologists from which particular era they originated. The drawback to relying on this method solely, without other tests, is that it may give inconclusive results because some tool designs carry over in time and can't be considered "time markers." In fact, archaeologists working on Anderson Marsh State Historic Park site have determined the relative age of the obsidian relics by incorporating a specialized process called obsidian hydration analysis. After first cutting a thin slice of the obsidian, the archaeologist observes it under a petrographic microscope. There the thickness of water bands on the outer surface of the artifacts is measured in microns, with a relative date of three microns equaling approximately 3,000 years.

Another method archaeologists use to determine dates of artifacts is by radiocarbon dating. Radiocarbon dating was developed by Willard F. Libby and associates in the 1940s when he won a Nobel Prize for his efforts. This method of dating is a way scientists can determine the age of artifacts by using a formula with the carbon-oxygen cycle. Radiocarbon dating is quite expensive, and is not used as frequently as the other methods mentioned. The artifacts discovered at Anderson Marsh State Historic Park were all processed at the Sonoma State University Hydration Lab.

There are over thirty known archaeological sites in Anderson Marsh some of which span 14,000 years. The Southeastern Pomo Indians, the furthest inland of the seven recognized Pomo language groups once lived on the land that is now Anderson Marsh. The archaeological sites represent habitation dating from 14,000 years before the present, to the early 20th century. By studying population patterns, scientists have hypothesized that in prehistoric times this area was more densely populated than any other area in California. There is evidence supporting the theory that a population density of about 15 people per square mile once inhabited the lands around Clear Lake. In many other regions, California Indian tribes required several square miles for a single person to subsist.

Archaeological surveys conducted by John Parker and David Fredrickson found that the Indians living here incorporated skilled hunting patterns and utilized the local environment's rich resources which included fish, birds and plant life. Foodstores could also include a variety of shellfish, waterfowl, small game, deer, acorns, tule shoots, bulbs and other roots, pine nuts, berries, and fruits.

Some of the park's numerous Native American archaeological sites were documented by the Lake County, California Cultural Heritage Council's Archaeological Field School. Coordinated by John Parker and using grant funds, students lived and worked on ancient sites. During this time clues were gathered and a past culture was reconstructed. Securing a National Endowment grant, John Parker directed an Anderson Marsh field school where groups of students and archaeologists camped out and learned traditional games, songs and dances. They worked on archaeological sites thousands of years old. Students garnered a feel for early Native Californian life and discovered firsthand which resources were available within walking distance. Here they were surrounded by the materials which met the early Native Californian's basic needs for food, shelter, clothing, and tools.

Historic Elements

Anderson Marsh has a designated historic period ranch complex (1855-1930), consisting primarily of the ranch house and two barns. The ranch complex also includes an early twentieth century smokehouse, a 1930s shed and corral with a loading chute, and a wooden, two-seater privy of the late nineteenth century. The ranch house is one of the few nineteenth century ranch homes remaining in Lake County which hasn't been significantly altered. It has been placed on the National Register of Historic Places. The ranch house's central section was constructed around 1855. It was built in the Greek Revival style of architecture. The west wing, or parlor section dates from the mid 1880s, and the east, or kitchen wing, from the 1920s. The kitchen section was built in the Craftsman Bungalow style, popular then.

The Andersons

Anderson Marsh derives its name from John Still Anderson, who bought the land from the California Agriculture Improvement Association, an affiliate of the Clear Lake Water Works

Company, in 1885. Anderson, a Scottish immigrant, operated a cattle ranch along with his wife, Sarah, and six children. The Andersons made a real home out of the small quarters. Today the house stands as a quiet reminder of times past. Special events such as the Blackberry Festival and tours are sometimes held to interpret the history of the ranch.

The Grigsbys

Prior to the Andersons settling the ranch, the Grigsbys, from Tennessee homesteaded here. In 1855 Achilles Fine, John Melchisadeck , and Tyrrel Lindsey Grigsby, brothers, built the central section of the house, along with a barn. It was here that John Melchisadeck Grigsby and his wife, Margaret Hale raised a family of one girl and nine boys. The Grigsbys raised livestock and agricultural produce. Tyrrell and Achilles lived in the Napa Valley. Another brother, Harrison, along with his wife and others on the wagon train died en route to California and were laid to rest in Bear Valley, Lake Tahoe. Later, their remains were brought to the Napa Valley, where they were buried in the Yountville cemetery.

Park Trails Overview

Anderson Marsh State Historic Park has four plant communities which are reflected in the park's five trails:

McVicar Trail

The McVicar Trail is a 3.5 mile walk that borders the park on the west boundary, leading to the shores of Clear Lake across from Indian Island. It takes you through grasslands and oaks. The trail was once called the McVicar Wildlife Sanctuary, as it was once owned by the National Audubon Society, and managed by the local branch called Redbud Audubon. This trail is a result of a Partnership Agreement between the Department of Parks and Recreation and the Anderson Marsh Interpretive Association. One hundred and fifty-one different species of birds have been identified in the park including the Lewis woodpecker, bald eagle, acorn woodpecker, and many more.

Cache Creek Trail

The Cache Creek Trail traverses a riparian environment. According to the California Department of Fish and Game, the park's valley oak riparian forest is one of only twenty-six left in the state. The valley oak forest and cottonwood-willow woodland comprises 4.5% of the park. The trail is 1.2 miles long. You can find migratory birds and pond turtles here.

Anderson Flats Trail

The Anderson Flats Trail leads through a grasslands environment. Due to grazing and cultivation, the grasslands habitat contains mainly non-native grasses. It covers 11% of the park. The trail is 0.8 miles long. In this area wildflowers and other seed-bearing plants can be found in abundance.

Ridge Trail

The Ridge Trail cuts through an oak woodland environment. This habitat makes up 7% of the park. The trail is 1.5 miles long. Blue oaks and many species of shrubs are found here. Animals such as the black-tailed deer, California ground squirrel, western gray squirrel, and other mammals inhabit this area. Birds such as the great horned owl, Cooper's hawk, woodpeckers, and other varieties of cavity-nesters inhabit this environment.

Park Trails Overview

Marsh Trail

The Marsh Trail allows for a panoramic vista of the park. The freshwater marsh habitat is predominant in the park, with 19% tule prairie and 42% sedge-rush prairie. The trail is 1.6 miles long. Bald eagles can be seen here during the winter months.

CACHE CREEK NATURE TRAIL

A walk here is to be savored, taken slowly and with concentration. I consciously slow my pace and breathe deeply, both figuratively and literally. The environment's effect on me is immediate. As I steep in the multi-hued landscape my senses heighten. Nature is contradictory in that she becalms and energizes one at the same time. My shoulders relax. When walking at an unhurried pace, the sound of leaves rustling, shadow of a turkey vulture, and a multitude of minutia reveal themselves to me. I look at nature's nuances as gifts. It becomes a game to walk a path I've taken many times and delight in the changes- sometimes subtle, sometimes overt- which have occurred since my last walk here.

I narrowly miss stepping on an ant hill, a thriving colony of industrious miniature creatures. Nearby a crack in the soil provides a cool, dark enclave for a spider who makes himself scarce when I cast a shadow and startle him back to his abode. I find that no two days are ever the same in Anderson Marsh. The thought compels me to wonder about the group of people who passed me earlier, adults chiding the children on. "Hurry up!" they pleaded, their perception blurred, no doubt by their need to be somewhere else. Poet William Blake said, "The tree which moves some to tears of joy is in the eyes of others only a green thing that stands in the way."

The Cache Creek Nature Trail begins behind the ranch house, past the blackberry patch. Blackberries typically ripen in August, when Anderson Marsh State Historic Park used to host the annual Blackberry Festival. Then, thousands of visitors arrived to take tours of the historic ranch house, participate in docent-led nature hikes and archaeological tours, they met descendants of the Andersons, and took in the old-timey atmosphere as park volunteers donned costumes from the turn of the nineteenth century. There was something for everyone: food, music, crafts, and booths of all description with people sporting turn-of-the-century garb, selling books, pottery and blackberry pies. The educational and entertaining Blackberry Festival might make a comeback by changing to a cooler calendar date, garnering more volunteers and more funding.

The ground creeping blackberry was indigenous to this area. The Himalayan blackberry, brought by a botanist to Massachusetts' Boston Botanical Gardens in 1870, is prevalent now, having "escaped" from the botanical gardens. By 1900 it took over western Washington. By 1940 it had become a pest in the Clear Lake area. Long before that, the blackberry was a useful plant for many California Indian tribes. Of course the sweet, juicy berries were consumed fresh when harvested in July or August, and they were sometimes dried and stored for later use. The root, obtained year-round, was used to alleviate diarrhea and other stomach ailments. The coastal Pomoans, known to us as the Kashaya Pomo Indians, believed that it was important that the berries not be eaten by pregnant women- or for that matter, the fathers-to-be. The Kashaya believed that their babies would be born dusky in color if berries were consumed during pregnancy.

The land which makes up Anderson Marsh State Historic Park was once the home of John Still Anderson and his family. The Cache Creek Nature Trail is cut through a field where the Andersons cultivated barley, wheat, and oats from 1885 to the 1960s. John Still Anderson (1834-1912) traveled from Edinburgh, Scotland with his wife, Sarah (1839-1916) and their six children: Grace (1865-1944), John Russell (1867-1938), Agnes (1870-1913), William (1871-1961), Charles (1874-1962) and Mora (1877-1966). Here is where they purchased about 1300 acres. Later, the Andersons purchased an additional 4,000 acres to graze their stock south of Cache Creek, in Morgan Valley.

Now, instead of the introduced varieties of barley, wheat and oats, the dominant plants are fat wild oat, or *Avena fatua*. Scientists believe that the fat wild oat seen here was hybridized and cultivated by aboriginal peoples. Interspersed with fat wild oat is curly dock (*Rumex crispus*), teasel (*Dipsacus fullonum*) and the ever-present invader, yellow star thistle. The unique-looking four-foot thistle, teasel was brought in to California by the Spaniards, via the Mission Trail. Indian slaves forced to work at the missions used teasel's sturdy head to card wool and as a comb.

When continuing along the trail it isn't long before the sunlit grainfields meet the banks of Cache Creek, the Clear Lake outlet channel. Here is where the Andersons once cultivated their vegetable garden. The garden was easily accessible to the ranch house and the nearby creek provided irrigation for their fruits and vegetables.

I have had the good fortune to meet several descendants

of the Anderson family who enraptured me with stories about ranch life, a way of living, which of course, included prolific gardening. I've met with Winifred Minden, born in 1913 and her brother Ted (John Theodore) Anderson, born in 1908. Winifred and Ted were John Still Anderson's grandchildren. They had two other brothers, Francis and Harold, as well as a sister, Lorna. Their father, John Russell Anderson and mother, Ianthe Carmen Baylis lived with their five children in a house just south of the ranch house on 40 acres. They attended school in the Lower Lake Schoolhouse, which is now the Lower Lake Schoolhouse Museum. The John Russell Anderson family moved about a quarter of a mile away sometime after 1914.

Winifred spoke fondly of days gone by when she used to visit her aunt, uncle, and other relatives at the ranch house. She recalls four o'clock was afternoon tea-time. I can almost smell the fresh-baked cookies, gingerbread, and cake baked by Winifred's aunt. The children were invited to play the piano. The original Anderson piano now holds a prominent spot in the Lake County Museum in Lakeport.

Once-common activities such as helping with the turkeys, chickens, and pigs, canning fruits and vegetables, and churning butter are now fondly reminisced. Winifred also spoke of the Anderson smokehouse (located behind the ranch house) where ham, bacon, and sausage were cured. Drinking water was obtained by a windmill-driven pump which was located northeast of the ranch house. Their apple orchard stretched across what is now State Highway 53. The Andersons, like most pioneers, made their own soap and generally lived off the bounty of the land.

Life was not easy during the early ranching days, however romantic it may seem to us now. Ted Anderson spoke of trying to keep coyotes and hawks from killing the chickens. When he was twelve years old, Ted went for a chicken hawk with a double-barreled shotgun. Needless to say, Ted was propelled backwards when the gun discharged, landing him flat on his bottom. Once he tried to prevent a coyote from dining on the chickens. This time he had a .22 caliber rifle, but shot the rooster instead! He was paid to trap skunks, as they were a hindrance to egg-production on the ranch, along with raccoons and foxes. Early one school day Ted trapped a skunk, then reluctantly made his way to school. He needn't have worried about attending school on that day because, as soon as he arrived, Ted was asked to leave. Apparently the teacher didn't care for the lingering aroma of skunk emanating from Ted's overalls! Other jobs Ted helped his family with at the ranch included picking the herb Yerba Santa to sell at the store in Lower Lake. Yerba Santa, a shrub which grows 20 to 40 inches tall and bears a multitude of white or lavender elongated flowers, was widely used by California Indians and pioneers as a cough medicine or "blood purifier." The leaves were gathered in summer and boiled to make a tea, and used as a poultice for sores.

Winifred recalled watching the ranch workers at cattle round-up time. The round-up was tough, dirty work which needed to be done so that the animals could be branded and earmarked. An earmark was a distinctive split made on a cow's ear to further aid in identifying one's own cattle. The Andersons owned over 350 red and white Polled Herefords. The "muleys" as the cattle were called, were driven by horseback all the way over Mt. St. Helena and down to Calistoga where they were collected by train to be sent for slaughter in San Francisco. By 1927 the cattle were driven by truck instead of train. Cattle and horses were vital to ranch operation. Each fall the whole field to the west of the ranch house and barn was worked by a team of horses pulling a plow.

The Anderson's hired help included Pomo Indians who were by that time relegated to a reservation across Cache Creek. The local Indian men helped with haying, which entailed mowing, raking, pitching, and bailing. Next, the hay wagon, drawn by two horses, was loaded up and the hay stored in the barns. Hay was important to life on the ranch. It was used to feed the ranch's six riding horses and six work horses. Some grain was sold, while some was used for seed. The Indian women worked on the ranch as well. They washed clothes in a large pot, their babies tucked safely away nearby in baby-carriers woven with the special basket weaving skills that Pomo Indians are famous for. It was typical for the men to attend to the more strenuous tasks such as construction, cattle chasing, branding, droving, bailing, raking, and pitching, while leaving the women to tend to tasks such as gardening, cooking, housekeeping, and tending the smaller livestock- the chickens, turkeys, and pigs.

The Anderson family maintained the ranch until 1964 when a family trust was formed. The ranch was then sold to Ray Lyons. Mora Anderson was the last Anderson to live at the ranch. She stayed on through a life estate agreement, living there until her death in 1966. The ranch was leased to Anthony Leonardini, Ray Lyons' brother-in-law. Leonardini raised cattle and grain there from 1964-82. Next, Dr. John Parker's quest to preserve this precious land began (detailed later in this book), and the rest, as they say is history.

The Cache Creek Nature Trail meanders along the edge of its namesake, Cache Creek, where several islands have formed, including Slater and Garner Islands. Slater Island was named for

William Slater, one of the first European Americans to inhabit the area. In 1856, Slater lived there with his wife, four daughters, two sons, and Mr. Jarvis Cable. Their home was actually located west of the ranch house.

The park's riparian community, running along Cache Creek and along Clear Lake, features an abundance of plant and animal life. The water's edge is shaded by lush willows, cottonwoods, valley oaks, and many shrubs. This habitat attracts red-shouldered hawks, warblers, American robins, wood ducks, great blue herons, mourning doves, a variety of hummingbirds, and other avian species. The area where land and water meet is rich in the insect-life that feeds the varied fish and bird species. It provides a nesting area for breeding waterbirds. The open riparian community is important for migratory birds who populate the area when they feed and rest along their strenuous journey. The wandering oxbows along Cache Creek provide shelter and resting places for black-tailed deer.

An 800 foot long bridge and boardwalk built in part by The Telephone Pioneers of America take me across one of the oxbows. Before crossing, I look down to the damp banks of the creek to try and "read" who's been here before me. If I'm lucky I'll see evidence of squirrel, raccoon, skunk, or opossums in the form of footprints in the wet soil. Crawdads, river otter, mink, muskrat, and gray fox have all been sighted as well. Today however, the terrain is illegible, and while looking away from the trail I startle a couple of frogs who dive off a log into the safety of the cool water below.

Further down the trail, I come upon a pair of glittering, jewel-like creatures: mating damselflies. They are beautiful circumpolar bluets. While damselflies mate on the ground, their relative, the dragonfly mates while flying. The primary difference between the damselfly and the dragonfly, I have learned, is that dragonflies hold their wings horizontally, like miniature airplanes, while damselflies place their wings to the back, vertically. The male of both species is territorial. When the female of his dreams flies into his territory, he holds her with his grasping organs which are located at the end of his tail. These insects are an important part of the food chain at the marsh. They consume mosquitoes and other flying insects. Large species of both dragon and damselflies eat tadpoles or fish. Dragonflies have the ability to grab their prey out of the air with their legs and devour it while flying as fast as thirty miles per hour. They are a boon to humans due to their ferocious appetites. The predacious dragonfly can consume its weight in insects in about a half an hour.

Dragonflies are known the world over, but those in South America are among the largest. Dragonflies in South America have a wingspan of seven inches. They took to the jungles at dusk when their pale, translucent wings reminded the native tribes of ghostly spirits. They are actually quite harmless to humans. They don't bite, sting, or dine on our crops. Besides emblazoning our environment with their effervescent beauty, dragonflies have played a part in the mythology of many lands. The Hopi Indians used the dragonfly symbol to adorn ceremonial pottery. To the Japanese the dragonfly symbolized victory in battle and they are widely featured in Japanese art and literature.

Odonata, the order to which dragonflies and damselflies belong has been around for over 300 million years. Fossil evidence tells us this. Long before the epoch of the early dinosaurs, dragonflies took to the skies with a wingspan of 36 inches, making them the largest of the flying insects. Imagine a time when the eighty-ton *Brachiosaurus* lumbered through tropical lagoons paying little attention to the giant dragonfly's graceful aerial path above the primeval mud.

A great blue heron ascends above me now. It gracefully glides overhead, wings like steady parasails. As it flaps its powerful wings steadily but slowly, its neck is held in a tight "S" shape. There is a heron rookery, or nesting site, in the oak trees on Slater Island which contains 30-40 active nests. The rookery is a lively, noisy place, contrasting sharply with the tranquility of the rest of the marsh. Great blue herons are territorial birds, and if their rookery is disturbed they will stop reproducing, and any displaced birds will not be accepted by herons in another nesting site. Herons dine on the plentiful fish, crustaceans, amphibians, insects, reptiles, and rodents found in the park. They have been known to consume the nestlings belonging to other bird groups as well.

Herons, and their relatives the bitterns and egrets, can be found throughout the world, with the exception of the Arctic regions and some islands. Our great blue heron stands about four feet high. The female lays from three to seven unspotted, pastel blue or green eggs. Both sexes care for the eggs, taking turns during the incubating process. The pair jointly care for their young, dutifully feeding via regurgitation until the young can fend for themselves, usually after about sixty days.

As the Cache Creek Trail gently winds away from the creek side, the cottonwood, willow, and oak make way for abundant vegetation up to the Ridge Point. Swaying tules, field pennycress, and cattail are thick here. If you're lucky, you may come upon a northwestern pond turtle, crayfish, or grebe at the shoreline.

Our continent floats like a water lily on a pond over earth's 1,800 mile thick not-quite-liquid, but not-quite-solid mantle, all the while tilted at 23.4 degrees on its axis. It is this tilt, caused by the sun and moon's gravitational pulls which results in seasons. If not for this tilt, Earth's days would all be equal in length and no seasons would occur, resulting, to say the least, in a very dull world. The climate of the past 10,000 years is known to have evolved from a steady, wet, cool climate to the present-day cool, wet winters and dry, hot summers. Locally, paleoclimactic research done on Clear Lake by using core samples indicates that the vegetation around the lake differed for the earliest tribes known to have inhabited the region. According to research compiled by Dr. John Parker, since the glacial period an increase in grasses and oaks is evident. The increase in grasses and oaks occurred between four and eight thousand years ago, or in paleoclimate terms, the Altithermal period. As mentioned in the introduction, Dr. Parker spearheaded the effort to create a state historic park out of Anderson Marsh. If it hadn't been for his lengthy and determined efforts, I doubt that our state would possess such a rich historical resource. Archaeologists like Parker have excavated manos and flat milling stones, which indicate seed grinding technology. Archaeologists tend to view the advent of this technology in several ways. Its use may be due to changes in climate, population, or availability of seeds. The pattern of setting up village sites near water sources such as streams, marshes, and lakes suggests that food from these places was abundant. Fish and fowl would probably have been the prevalent dietary sources. Either grasses became more abundant, or food from the water sources declined. There is the possibility that both occurred. Archaeologists hypothesize that with a more sizable food supply a population increase follows, increasing the need for larger food supplies. The native population would then find it necessary to procure other resources.

At the end of the Altithermal climatic period was the Middle Archaic Period of three to four thousand years ago. Archaeologists have noted a change in projectile point styles at this time. Mortar and pestle tools were associated with the tribes of two to three thousand years ago in the area, during a period known to archaeologists as the Upper Archaic. Mortar and pestle were utilized primarily for grinding acorn and nuts. Tools, beginning as large spear points, including Folsom and Clovis points of ten to twelve thousand years ago, and Borax Lake points of four to eight thousand years ago evolved to the use of atlatl, darts, and the smaller bow and arrow points. Archaeologists classify the various spear and arrow points into type by shape. Some may be leaf-shaped, some with concave bases, or notched corners for fastening onto spears. The materials used, as well as their shapes help archaeologists piece the puzzle of their place in time together.

Geologic resources that were important to the area's inhabitants for tool-making include Konocti and Borax Lake obsidian. The mountains around Lake County are actually a metamorphic formation of the Cretaceous period. The Franciscan geologic formation which surrounds the Clear Lake basin includes other rocks which were employed by the Native population in the making of stone tools: steatite, magnesite, and chert. The Franciscan rock unit also hosts sediments which consist of sandstone and chert interspersed with basalt lava. Chert was important in Pomoan tool manufacture. Chert comes from the crystallization of the skeletons of microscopic animals, and is usually brown, red, or green.

Serpentinite, California's state rock, is a common geologic

feature in the vicinity. It is green and can be speckled with black. As it is shiny, it is sometimes confused with jade. To confuse matters further, serpentinite and jade can be found in the same rock formation. Jade is much heavier and harder than serpentinite. Jade can also be distinguished from serpentinite by a light tap with a rock hammer. The harder jade will not break, while the softer serpentinite will crumble when tapped. Unique and beautiful minerals can be found in abundance around the lake, where there is much evidence of volcanic activity. For example, you can find pumice and obsidian in great quantities. The mineral, borax can be found near Lake County's Borax Lake. In 1864, the lake was worked by W.S. Jacks of Napa for the California Borax Company. Borax was prized for its detergent and water-softening qualities, and is still used today as a flux for welding and soldering.

Native Americans ingeniously utilized the materials found in their territories. Contrary to what many Euro-historians wrote in the late 1800s about the Native American population, these were complex societies with organization in all aspects of their lives. The villages had their own governing councils and set up political boundaries. Native societies of the Clear Lake area traded with neighboring tribes as far away as the Pacific coast. Due to the climate and geographic boundaries, the Pomo became trade specialists. Cooperation between tribes like this suggests that diversification of food resources was important at this time. Due to the extensive trade, Mount St. Helena had footpaths worn into its surface from regular use by Native American travelers. Those designated to travel would trade local obsidian for prized shells, seaweed, and sometimes fish. Some of the shells were used in the Pomoan monetary system and made into beads, which became an important commodity.

Headmen of each tribe wore large strands of beads to designate wealth. Through the use of reconstructed pumpdrills, the tool utilized to make the beads, it has been found that most people can make clamshell beads, however not in the aesthetically round and well-proportioned fashion reminiscent of a true craftsman. Beads are not easy to make, and require a lot of time to do so. Bead manufacture was a specialized occupation. The shells utilized were predominantly *Macoma* and Washington clam shell, with some use of abalone, mussel, and *Olivella* shell. When the shells were collected, they were broken into pieces. Next, they were smoothed into disc-shapes by rubbing the shells on the rough surface of a stone. The hole in the bead was then drilled. After the beads were strung, they were smoothed into uniform and rounded shapes. Clam shell bead manufacturing occurred during the Emergent Period of A.D. 500 to historic contact times of about 1820. Interestingly, Pomos sometimes traded magnesite as well. Bead cylinders fashioned from the valuable mineral were said to have been worth many times their length in shell beads. The magnesite bead's color was enhanced by firing it in a manzanita wood fire. The mineral was obtained from eastern Lake County.

The bow and arrow, along with the hopper mortar were in evidence during the Emergent Period. The hopper mortar was an ingenious method of processing acorns into meal by incorporating a hole in a flat stone and attaching a hopper (or basket) to it which was held secure by pressure or cement. Pomos are well known for the variety, versatility, and beauty of their basketry. In fact, they are considered to be the best basket-makers in the world. To prepare for basket weaving women gathered a variety of materials, including redbud branches, bulrush roots, sedge grasses, and willow. Elaborate baskets incorporating beads, feathers, and intricate designs, were given as gifts and used in religious ceremonies. The red feathers used on some baskets came from woodpeckers, yellow-colored feathers came from orioles, while green feathers were obtained from mallard ducks. Baskets were used every day for carrying babies, trapping fish, and for the storage and gathering of seeds. Baskets were even used to cook in! Baskets could be woven so tightly that they could hold water. A meal could be cooked in a basket by placing very hot cooking stones into the soup with a specially made cooking utensil. To avoid scorching the basket, the rocks were constantly stirred until the meal was ready to eat. Pottery sherds with white willow basket imprints have been found in recent years, which indicate some baskets in this area were lined with clay to help them hold water.

The people who once inhabited the marsh were both hunter-gatherers and horticulturists due to their practice of utilizing their environment for maximum yield via control burns. In times past, the native peoples winnowed grass seed from this prolific valley floor. After the grass seed was harvested, the enterprising Indians dug holes at intervals throughout the meadow, approximately one and one-half feet deep, then burned the field. The parched seed was re-collected, then ground, and finally cooked into a bread or mush. This control burn served many purposes. It killed undesirable plants, enriched the soil with ash, and it protected the village from wildfire. As an added bonus the mice and shrew which had taken refuge in the strategically located holes were collected, ground up, bones and all, then savored as a delicacy.

The Indians residing in the Clear Lake basin retained their traditional lifestyle for a longer period of time than did the tribes residing on the coast along the Spanish Mission trail. Because they resided at an inland location, at a considerable distance from the Spanish missions, the Indians in this area weren't forcibly removed from their homelands until approximately the 1830s. Other California Indian tribes were forced to work at the missions as early as 1769, when the mission in San Diego, San Diego de Alcala, was founded. The northern most mission in the recognized California mission chain, San Francisco Solano, in Sonoma County, was founded in 1823. Ethnographic records and archaeological evidence show that tribes around Anderson Marsh endured forced removal to General Mariano Vallejo's Petaluma Adobe, and were coerced into slave labor, with some being tortured and sent to other ranches. The arrival of a Spanish priest to Lake County, Father Lucian Osuna, in 1867 didn't have the impact on native peoples that the colonization of the coast by the twenty-one Franciscan missionaries had. Father Osuna's mission operations were smaller, requiring fewer Indians to work it. According to Lake County historian Henry Mauldin, Father Osuna was believed to belong to the Franciscan Order. Before the arrival of Father Osuna, Catholic services had previously been held in a district schoolhouse on Kelsey Creek. In 1867, a permanent mission was built on the shores of Clear Lake, three miles north of Kelseyville. Mission St. Turibius, as it was called, was situated on 235 acres, and served as both church and school. Later, Indians from the surrounding area including Big Valley established a Catholic Indian settlement called the Rancheria of St. Turibius Mission. Up to twenty homes were constructed for the 60 to 100 Indians who lived on the mission. Father Luciano Osuna left Lake County in 1878, and other Franciscan Fathers ran the mission until 1881. When the Franciscan Fathers who replaced Father Osuna left the mission, a spate of new religious leaders took their places: The Fathers of the Holy Cross presided over the mission from 1881-83, and the Society for the Propagation of the Faith were in charge from1883-87. The Franciscan Fathers returned for an undetermined amount of time after that. Many Indians remained at the mission until 1914, when they moved to the newly established United States Government Big Valley Rancheria one mile from Finley.

The fabric of Native American life changed enormously in Lake County. Hard-working European families came to California by the thousands, thereby altering the land forever. The Indian population in pre-European time in California was estimated to be 300,000 in 1769. The population declined to 30,000 by 1860. This was the beginning of the end of thousands of years of a lifeway that the Pomo people knew.

In 1834 General Mariano Guadalupe Vallejo was in command of the Mexican forces north of San Francisco Bay, and headquartered in the Presidio in Sonoma, where he was sent to secularize the mission. He placed his brother, Captain Salvador Vallejo, and Captain Ramon Corrillo in charge of the exploration of the Clear Lake area in 1836. Salvador Vallejo then applied for a Mexican Land Grant of sixteen leagues, which included land in Upper Lake, Bachelor Valley , Big Valley, and Scott's Valley. It hasn't been proven that this land was ever officially ceded to him. Nevertheless, Salvador's brother, the Comandante General of the Government was "the law", and his brother took possession. In 1841 Salvador Vallejo had a Southeastern Pomo Indian village massacred by Mexican troops when they refused to come to Napa Valley to harvest grain. That wasn't the last of the atrocities. Charles Stone and Andrew Kelsey purchased stock from Salvador Vallejo about that time, and garnered permission to use his land for grazing. Kelsey and Stone used the local Native Americans as slave labor to build an adobe house. It was common knowledge in the nearby settlements that Stone and Kelsey mistreated Native Americans to the extreme. The Native Americans were not fed and forced to labor harder and harder if they complained. They were whipped, beaten, and horribly abused. They could no longer tolerate the hunger and beatings, so they killed some cattle to eat. This incident did not sit well with Stone and Kelsey. Many events ensued- one Native American was tied to a tree then beaten, some Native's homes were burned down, and others were marched to the gold fields where all but one or two met with malaria and died. Added to those heartrending incidents was the fact that Chief Augustine's wife was kidnapped and forced to live with the white men. So, in the fall of 1849 Stone and Kelsey were murdered by Native Americans- Kelsey with an arrow, Stone by way of a blow to the head with a rock. In the spring of 1850 a detachment of United States soldiers led by Captain Lyons was sent from the San Francisco Presidio or Benicia with whale-boats hauled by wagons, along with cannons, in retaliation for Stone and Kelsey's deaths. Pomo peoples fishing on what is now called Bloody Island, in Clear Lake were targeted and massacred by the troops. Women and children were killed indiscriminately- soldiers chased them into the water, bludgeoning and shooting them. This massacre was replayed again and again over the course of a month as the soldiers continued killing Northern and Central Pomo Indians, working their havoc westward toward Ukiah. It is believed that one of the cannons hauled by Lyons' troops may be buried at Anderson Marsh. Another cannon went to its watery grave in the depths of Clear Lake, and one was left at the base of Mt. Konocti. The United States government concluded its tyranny in 1851 by drafting a treaty and trying to initiate a reservation. Throughout this time Euro-American settlements sprang up, and their cattle changed the landscape and lifestyle of the Native culture forever.

> If you tie a horse to a stake, do you expect he will grow fat? If you pen an Indian up on a small spot of earth, and compel him to stay there, he will not be contented, nor will he grow and prosper. I have asked some of the great white chiefs where they get their authority to say to the Indian that he shall stay in one place, while he sees white men going where they please. They cannot tell me. Chief Joseph , Nez Perce leader, Cedar Falls, Iowa, April 1879.

The oblique sunlight of the late afternoon shines like a diluted version of itself through the wispy cloud cover. Nature is more subtle and subdued in her choice of color late in the day, near the end of the winter season. The riotous wildflowers and jewel-green of spring are things of the past. Through looking more carefully, by-passing the broad view, and concentrating on individual trees, bushes, and hills, I begin to discern a wider range of color. The hills beyond the marsh appear in purple hues. The mistletoe stands out velvety, verdant, and proud against the bare oak branch. The vast landscape beckons me and incites a passion to know and understand its extensive composition. It challenges me to experience and examine its sights, sounds, and smells- no mean feat considering what extravagance I stand upon.

Ridge Trail

Once off of State Highway 53 and onto the state park grounds, you don't have to walk far to leave the twentieth century behind. If the ancient earth here could speak, it would communicate its perpetual story of the Southeastern Pomo. Prior to evidence produced by modern research methods, anthropologists referred to many Northern California Indian tribes as one group. Many cultural similarities occurred between the tribes, but there were distinct differences between the languages. W.W. Gifford, anthropologist, learned of dialects and subdialects in the various Pomo villages. For instance, in the area around Clear Lake, Southeastern and Eastern Pomo languages were spoken in the tribes. Other Pomoan languages named for their geographic locations are Central Pomo, Northern Pomo, Southwestern Pomo, Southern Pomo, and Northeastern Pomo. Gifford believed that the Southeastern Pomo, who dwelled on the land around Anderson Marsh, had family-owned parcels, while the Eastern Pomo who inhabited the Upper Lake area didn't own specific land parcels. The Southeastern Pomo was broken into three political divisions, or tribelets: Koi, Elem, and Kamdot. Koi village was situated on what is now Anderson

Marsh. Important connections were maintained between the various tribes, as they traded, sometimes intermarried, and participated in important ceremonies together.

Until 1997 there was a Pomo Indian round house exhibit on the knoll at the park. The round house was located on one of the few sites in the park that isn't archaeologically sensitive. The round house was considered to be the political, religious, and ceremonial center of the Indian village. The construction of the roundhouse in 1987 was to assist in the preservation of the Pomo Indian culture so that their customs could be shared with people of all cultures. It was a fine and worthy project, and it is hoped by many that local Native Americans will find an appropriate way; i.e. one that is sensitive to their culture and needs, to bring their past alive for school children and others who are eager to learn about an important part of California history.

The trail I follow has been cut through a mix of native and introduced grasses, interspersed with that obnoxious intruder, yellow star thistle. Yellow star thistle found its way to California along with the population surge of the gold rush era. The plant was a hitchhiker from southern Europe around 1849, firmly establishing itself in Lake County fields in the 1970s. It thrives during the hottest weeks of summer.

Summer is a determined season. Determined not to be overlooked by spring's grand showings of wildflowers, and new-born life of all description. Summer stretches out into languorous, albeit hot, glorious days. In summer you still find vivid blossoms and all of the sybaritism of the finest spring day. Summer season actually causes quite a commotion, for nature has appointed her creatures great and small with an abundant means of communication. One way we learn about this is through bioacoustics: the science that traces sounds animals make among themselves. These sounds remain hidden from us without the use of elaborate equipment but form musical harmony throughout the animal kingdom. Amazingly, sounds are emitted from the smallest species, such as the drumming-in-their-nests of termites, on up the scale to the largest whale-song. We're all aware of birdsong, a coyote howling, and the unmistakable sound of the rattlesnake, but the sounds deciphered by bioacoustics that were unknown until relatively recently include the clicks and bell tones of bats and the ticking of certain types of beetles. And who would have thought of fish as noise-makers? They have been found to make clicking noises with their teeth.

Summer is also a decidedly sensuous season. Sensuous in that all of one's senses seem to be more acute. The annual miracles that nature performs don't dull with repetition, but quite to the contrary, seem to be taken less for granted as each year passes. I drink in the organic odor and texture of earth in my vegetable garden. Mycelium, the vegetal, threadlike part of fungus, is busy breaking down and composting leaf mold. Bacteria and moisture aid in this never-ending process, resulting in rich humus. Flowers which suspended their growth during winter and relied on starches in their bulb roots have muscled their way up and out of the earth. Insects and grubs busy themselves in underground tunnels- their eternal nocturnal habitat. Summer sunshine evaporates the shiny morning dew quickly as the thermometer rises, and works her magic deep into earth's crust. The annual nesting of birds taking place nearby is, to me, reassuring. A feeling of "all is as it should be" occurs as I watch them painstakingly build a nest from scratch with blades of dried grasses. Their homes are built as a result of the direct stimuli to their biological systems triggered by the changing of the seasons, such as rainfall, temperature, and length of day.

The landscape at Anderson Marsh has retained its contour of a hundred years ago. There are undulating hills of grasses, oaks, scrub, and pine as far as the eye can see. I want to know the name of each and every plant I come in contact with. I consult my guide books. I want to know the language of the land. I mentally "pull up a chair," as another show has begun: A killdeer slightly larger than a robin, heaves down on its prey- a grasshopper, and jostles the aerial inflorescence of a dandelion crown. A fleet of delicately drifting parachutes is released; the downy seeds free to meet their destiny far from home. I'm amazed once again by the sheer beauty of what occurs throughout this land on a daily basis. Walt Whitman once said, "In this broad earth of ours, amid the measureless grossness and the slag, enclosed and sage within its central heart, nestles the seed perfection."

A Pomo trickster myth concerning small birds and the mythological character, Coyote, comes to mind: Coyote, while walking south, came across a place where there were many small birds. Seeing Coyote, they fled into the brush. Coyote asked the birds why they fly that way, into the thick bushes. A bird told him that they fly in that manner in order to express their happiness. The bird then began to explain the procedure to Coyote in detail. While one bird was giving Coyote instructions, the others were constructing small, sharp sticks to place in the brush. The bird then asked Coyote if he would like to try it. He was more than willing, so the birds each gave him a feather, placed them all over Coyote's body, and then showed him where to fly into the brush like the birds. Coyote unwittingly flew into the brush. He was caught in their trap; a stick poked out his eye. He begged for help, so Tree gave him some moss for his eye. Soon, Blue Jay came by and doctored Coyote, helping his eye to return to normal. While Blue Jay was administering help, he explained to Coyote the reason for such bad luck. Blue Jay said, "You are a good hunter, but you never give a feast. You must remember that next time." Then Coyote left Blue Jay for his homeward journey.

Nature's nighttime show is equally enchanting and absorbing. For instance, the Clear Lake basin is home to many bats. Among them are: The western big-eared bat, pallid bat, big brown bat, little brown bat, long-eared bat, fringed bat, and California myotis. Bats, mammals which occur world-wide, have a negative reputation as depicted in legends and myths. Contrary to stories told at late-night campfires however, bats are generally beneficial to humans, consuming insects, pollinating plants, and aiding in seed dispersal. Bats have the distinction of being the only mammal gifted with the ability of prolonged flight. In the suborders of bats there are microbats and megabats. Megabats in India and Africa grow to a wingspan of over five feet, while on the other end of the scale, Thailand boasts the tiniest microbat- the kitti, which is a little over an inch long.

One of the most common bats to our area, the big brown bat, *Eptesicl fuscus*, has a twelve-inch wingspan. Big brown bat's fur is long and glossy. Like most bats, its wings are actually thin membranes supported by long bones, enabling it to aerodynamically lift to navigate and find prey. Echolocation, or emitting high-frequency sound which is bounced back as echoes to their ears, helps bats determine distance and position throughout the darkest of nights. Big Brown Bat prefers crevices or caves as its habitat. Its diet consists wholly of insects. Like other bats, it roosts during the day, hanging upside down by its feet.

Little brown bat, *Myotis lucifugus*, is often associated with caves, hollow trees, or timbered areas. Its glossy upperpart is cinnamon in color, while the bat's underpart is pale gray. They are very common and can often be spotted in the late afternoon or dusk winging their way over water, or dining near the woods.

The pallid bat found here is a relatively large bat, with a forearm of over two inches. This bat has twenty-eight teeth which are used to feed on insects caught on the ground. These bats range in color from light brown to yellowish, with the darker bats usually being found on the northwest coast, and the more pale colored bats residing in the desert. Both sexes of these migratory bats spend their days roosting together in small openings, barns or crevices.

Other nocturnal creatures include the owls. Once I startled a great horned owl, or rather, we startled one another. It swooshed out of the oak tree near the vernal pool located just over the fence line south of the park.

The vernal pool, a miniature ecosystem, and protected by law, is home to specific plants which thrive only in the rarified environment. Vernal pools are depressions which are found in grasslands and fill with water each year. The floor of the vernal pool is hardpan and often dries by late spring. Many vernal pools have been found in the counties of Napa, Merced, Solano, and Placer. Prehistoric artifacts like manos (loaf-shaped grinding stones), pestles, and millingstones have been unearthed by vernal pools in those counties. Archaeologists think that vernal pools were prime locations for prehistoric campgrounds, as plants associated with these pools provided important foods for the various tribes. The vernal pool here may have enticed some delectable prey to the vicinity of the owl, whose diet consists entirely of other living animal species. Although it swooped down near me during the day, most owls are nocturnal birds. They possess mighty talons, designed to grasp their prey, and don't hesitate to defend their territory. Their wingspan reaches a whopping eighty inches. A unique characteristic of the owl is that they have a bone called the sclerotic ring surrounding their eyes. This bone allows for very little eye movement. However, because they have the ability to turn their heads 270 degrees, they don't have to miss a thing. Some species of owls have ears which are located asymmetrically on their heads. One ear higher than the other enables them to pinpoint sound with a great degree of accuracy. It surprised me to learn that all owls lay snow-white eggs. One would think that with two families and about 181 species, there would be some variation in the coloration of the eggs they lay. Another unique feature about owls is their "leftovers" from dinner. Owls consume their prey lock, stock, and barrel, or rather- hair, feathers, and bone but those portions of the meal being indigestible are neatly packaged into an "owl pellet;" a compacted, oblong parcel that is regurgitated by the owl. A friend once found some owl pellets beneath her tree, then gave them to me. I took them to my fourth grade class where we donned surgical gloves and proceeded to dissect the pellets. It was fascinating to see all manner of hair and neatly discarded mouse bones within the pellet package.

Throughout long, dark evenings, the Pomo Indians told many, many stories using the night and all of its celestial bodies as the protagonists. In the myth translated in Northern Pomo dialect and collected by S.A. Barrett, "Coyote Creates the Sun, Moon and Stars and Peoples the Earth," Coyote peeled the bark from four sticks of pine and prepared them with eagle and buzzard feathers, attaching them with string from a milkweed plant.

Next, he positioned himself in four ways- laying on his stomach, standing upon his head, laying on his back, and standing up straight. Then he scattered water up to the sky by flinging a dipper of water about. After a timespan of four days, clouds formed sufficiently as to gradually cover the sky. Coyote then took an obsidian knife, cut four corners into an oak ball and tossed it up high where it became the sun. The sun told the moon that it would like her for his mother. The moon, having been created in an earlier myth told by the Pomo, was created out of blue clay. The sun and the moon said that Coyote should make a fire, then throw the glowing coals up into the sky to create the stars. They said he should be sure to send another one up toward the east to create the morning star. Coyote asked Mother, "How can we make it dark?"

Moon said, " Well, we will make a big fire and we will then take a willow club and strike it and make it go out. That will make it dark."

The Sun promised two things: It promised that it would never go out, and that it would rise each morning. The Moon then said that he would shake his head to make the earth quake. Meanwhile, Coyote stated that he wanted to continue creating things. So he designed plants, food, birds, and animals, giving each a specific job and place to dwell. Coyote promised to always live in the mountains, even if it meant he could get killed doing so. The creation of the plants and animals took him two days and two nights. After these he fashioned supernatural beings which took another two days and two nights. It took a total of eight days for Coyote to create everything. Having done so, Coyote decided to go home and rest.

The Ridge Trail guides me through the powers of the wilderness via unseen but telling voices. I can hear the soft, short notes of a Lewis woodpecker- the anthem of the woods. The summer breeze allows every leaf to speak out. As I travel the trail beneath interlacing tree branches, each tree and shrub unique unto itself, I feel the impact of the land. It urgently calls my attention. Savoring the cool and pleasant shade I feel honored by the gentle, old oaks. They impart a tentative majesty through their immense presence, and command respect. Their moss-covered trunks and twisting limbs seem to harbor the secret memories, aeons old, which I desire to know. The blue oaks here are resistant to drought and thrive in a hot, dry climate. Blue oaks are known to be one of the most resilient and tolerant of all of the oaks, according to Cachuma Press and California Oak Foundation's, *Oaks of California*. Their roots grow at a more rapid rate than those of other oak varieties. Being smaller at maturity and possessing a unique coating on their leaves reinforces their survival rate. The leaves of this deciduous oak produce a wax-like covering on the upper surface of their leaves, assisting the canopy's water conservation and contributing to the blue oak's characteristic color. If the wax mechanism isn't sufficient, the tree has another drought-tolerant trick up its sleeve. In the event that soil beneath the tree becomes too dry, the foliage beefs up its leaves with wood-like substances, lignin and cellulose. If drought conditions are extreme, the tree goes dormant, usually until the following spring. Blue oak, also known as mountain white oak or iron oak was named by Scottish botanical explorer David Douglas who lived from 1798 to 1834.

By keeping to the trail, I am sure to avoid poison oak, which causes a red, itchy rash on those who are allergic. Poison oak, not related to the oak family, is related to the cashew family. It is easily recognizable by its shiny, lobed leaves of three. This perennial shrub produces white to yellowish berries during the summer or fall months. According to some accounts, aboriginal peoples were not affected by poison oak. Some Native Americans used poison oak to wrap around acorn meal. Also, the juice produced a black dye which was incorporated into the basketmaking process. The coastal, or Kashaya Pomoans made a tattooing paste from ashes of burnt poison oak. The uses of the plants indigenous to California were many and varied. Plant gathering of any kind was never taken for granted. There were almost as many cultural uses for plants as there were plants themselves. In many cultures, the Kashaya Pomo in particular, it was taboo or strictly forbidden for a menstruating woman and her husband to gather plants for food or other uses. A special respect was solemnly exhibited in the form of a prayer or song offered to the Creator for plants taken from their environment. The person gathering herbs or food explained to the Creator why it was necessary to take the plants before harvesting them. It was customary and necessary for the gifts from the earth to be shared, or homage paid in some other form like a ceremonial dinner.

Once, when I took a guided walk along the McVicar Audobon trail just past the Ridge Trail, the guide pointed out a porcupine napping in a tree. While everyone else could readily observe its pincushion form, a rare privilege, it took me quite some time to decipher it. It inconspicuously snoozed high above the wooded floor, its light-tipped quills creating the perfect camouflage. Once I saw it, it was difficult to understand why I hadn't been able to see it before. Windows on the world; our sight is the most dominant sense we humans possess. Our brains are kept super busy decoding what we see. Scientists have determined that about two-thirds of our brain's power concerns itself with visual interpretation. Our eye's seven million cone cells see colors and the most intricate details, however, they don't work in the dark. When nighttime scenery "grays out," the rods in our eyes take over.

Mirages defy the axiom, "seeing is believing." Sometimes sighted by those who are extremely thirsty, or under great strain, the phenomenon is frequently seen on hot highways or deserts. The heat from the ground radiates, causing a dense layer of air to hover just above it, which in turn acts like a lens, bending light to produce the appearance of water. We "see" in many different ways. For example we see in our mind's eye via memory and imagination. If we close our eyes we can still "see" form, color, and distance. We can envision things, and then bring them to pass. Many people are visual learners. Howard Gardner's Theory of Multiple Intelligences states that there are eight- and probably many more, ways people learn, with the visual-spatial intelligence being a predominant method of learning for the majority of people. The other intelligences are: verbal-linguistic, logical-mathematical, bodily-kinesthetic, musical-rhythmic, interpersonal, intrapersonal, and naturalist. Most people learn best with a combination of intelligences.

I am hiking through a variety of shrubs along the Ridge Trail now. Skunkbrush, California rose, and redbud commingle with other greenery, settling into the scene. Among the broad fringe I discern the western redbud, a plant of great significance for both the modern-day Pomoan basket weavers and their ancestors. This vigorous shrub can reach six to fifteen feet in height with a luxuriance of smooth, rounded, and glossy leaves. The magenta-pink flowers of spring contrast with the green herbage and call for attention. The bark from the redbud's switches provide the brown design in baskets, or may be peeled to reveal the milky white coloration if desired.

Flowers like those on the redbud naturally attract bees and other winged, flower- feeding insects. The pollen found in flowering plants provides a source of protein for both the bee and their larvae, while the plant's oils and nectars are utilized as a source of energy. The relationship between bee and flower is a classic case of symbiosis: The pollen feeds the bees, while the bee unwittingly contributes to the pollination process. In fact, bees are the most valuable pollinating insects of the insect world. By disturbing or spilling pollen which the bees have collected for their own use, enough of the golden fluff lands on the flower's pistils (or reproductive structures) to cause pollination of the plant to occur- mutualism extraordinaire. Scientists have determined that there are at least 20,000 species of bees in the world, and probably many more that have yet to be discovered. The honeybees most commonly seen in Lake County are a European bee, but species of small "native" bees can still be found, both locally, and in the United States. Bees inhabit almost all corners of the world, with the exception of places with extremely high altitude, the North and South Poles, and some oceanic islands. Africanized honeybees, deemed "killer bees" have been spreading northward from Brazil since 1956, when they were introduced from Africa. Arriving in California in 1994, they have been sighted as far west as Campo, a small town east of San Diego, California. The aggressive bees are dreaded due to their painful, repeated, and sometimes deadly stings. Agriculture experts in California's vital Central Valley feel that the killer bees pose a threat to their hardworking honeybees and the part they play in pollinating the state's $24 billion agricultural industry. The wet spring of 1998, El Nino, is blamed for the killer bee's push into the northern deserts. Killer bee task forces and entomologists are teaming up to devise strategies for containing the thriving colonies of bees. Deterrents to the unwanted species may include cross-breeding with more docile bees. It is believed that cross-breeding may dilute the killer bee's gene pool. Cold winters may play a part in deterring the proliferation of the aggressive bees as well.

Manzanita (*Arctostaphylos columbiana*) is outstanding with its rich brown branches and dense crown of brilliant green foliage. Soon it will be laden with exquisite clusters of white bells. The fallen blooms will then luxuriously carpet the ground below the shrub. The plant grows from three to twenty-five feet high, but according to *The Wild Flowers of California* by Mary Elizabeth Parsons, the largest manzanita known is thirty-five feet tall, and can be found in St. Helena, California.

Like its relative the madrone, the manzanita's bark unfurls like papery cinnamon-sticks, revealing a smooth new surface. The Spanish named the manzanita, which means "little apple," and refers to the shrub's berries. The berries ripen during July and August, their robust red color enhanced by the brilliance of the plant's green foliage. The Native American population made good use of the abundant manzanita: The berries were gathered for cider, eaten raw, or dried, ground, and cooked in a mush or bread. The leaves were sometimes used to aid in healing sores, and for other valuable purposes.

I take advantage of the cooling shade of a massive, old oak tree. It has been determined that this impressive valley oak is four to five hundred years old. By the looks of its acorn-studded bark it has been a popular acorn woodpecker cache for quite some time.

According to O*aks of California* oak trees belong to the genus *Quercus*. There are 18 species of oak in California, and possibly 500 worldwide. In our state's ancient past we had an even larger variety of oak species. Scientists have found rich records etched in fossils, proof that oaks once proliferated throughout the mountains, valleys, and plains, gracing millions of acres with their magnificence. Architecturally, oaks are remarkably designed. Because they love light and stretch out to embrace it, their canopy creates plenty of shade to discourage competition. The creation of shade lowers soil temperatures on the ground below, encouraging survival even in the extreme heat of summer. Its ability to defy gravity by bringing up water molecules which cling together, forming a water column through its vessels is unlike that of tall, straight trees. The oak's broad expanse of multiple branches allows for the cohesion-tension process to sidestep the greater forces of gravity placed on much taller trees, so that the capillary action moves water up from root to leaf with greater efficiency. The wide-body design of an oak is conducive to a greater durability. That, coupled with its massive root structure, which actually surpasses the length and width of the tree itself, generates a stabilizing effect during inclement weather.

The stalwart oak seedling begins its life by producing a prominent taproot from the acorn. The acorn is actually the tree's fruit, developing from the female oak flower's ovary. Through the miraculous powers within, the taproot grows and thickens. Meanwhile, other powerful processes are taking place- the root becomes gravity-sensitive and begins to push down and into the nourishment of the soil. After a length of about five feet the taproot ceases growing. Now, the lateral roots begin their mighty job of storing food for the tree. Feeder roots multiply, making a mammoth maze of underground networks, allowing for the oak's rapid growth to take place.

Competition for the acorns is stiff, with hungry birds, mammals, and insects all vying for the nutrient-rich fruit's fats, proteins, and carbohydrates stored within its smooth hull. As if the odds of surviving predation weren't enough, the acorn's fight for survival isn't over. For germination to take place there needs to be sufficient autumn or winter rains. The acorns need to fall to a place that provides enough sunlight, beyond the shade of their immense parents. However, if the conditions are too hot, germination will not occur. The naturally occurring detritus of the oak woodland floor provides a nutritious as well as safe habitat for the embryo root's job ahead- to push through the decaying acorn husk and begin the lengthy process mapped out in its genetic makeup long ago.

Of all of the oak varieties found in California, the valley oak is considered to be the most regal. Many trees reach heights surpassing 100 feet, with trunks over six feet in diameter. The record-holder for the valley oak with the largest trunk diameter has to be the ancient specimen near Gridley, Butte County, whose trunk is 9.3 feet in diameter. The valley oak's name is taken from where they can usually be found- in rich, fertile valleys. Under ideal conditions some valley oaks have been found to reach 600 years of age. These ancient monarchs had to survive disease, drought, fire, wind, and the perils of modern agriculture. As more and more land is cleared for agricultural and residential development valley oaks have been slowly disappearing from our landscape. As these stately trees are part of California's heritage, steps are being taken to guard against their complete obliteration. The California Oak Foundation is promoting the statewide protection of oaks. They are a nonprofit organization working to protect, conserve, and perpetuate California's native oak woodlands. They strive to educate decision-makers and the general public about the importance of our state's oak woodlands, watersheds, and wildlife habitat.

Oak trees remain at risk despite Proposition 117 which, according to *Oaks of California,* allocated monies in 1990 for 30 years for the purpose of enhancing oak communities and their wildlife habitats. Since California's population has swelled to about 30 million and continues to grow, the need to recognize the recurring loss of California's oaks is vital. Preservation depends largely on decisions being made on private lands.

The Pomo Indians of times past favored the variety of acorn produced by the black oak. If the season was good to them, they would gather up the abundant acorns when dry. Sometimes acorns were collected from the trees by striking the branches until the acorns dropped or by cutting down acorn-laden branches. Large, conical baskets carried on their backs and held by a forehead strap were used for acorn-gathering. As many as 400-500 pounds (or eight basketfuls) would supply a family for a year. Next, they hulled the acorn and ground the bitter meat by using a pestle and mortar. Another functional basket was employed during the pulverizing process. The basket was bowl-shaped, but bottomless. It fit the mortar precisely. The purpose of this unique basket was to provide a hopper, allowing more acorns to be processed at one time. A common sound could be heard coming from the villages during the time of acorn grinding: the thumping of the pestle to grind the staff of life. Leaching was next. By leaching, the meal was divested of tannin and glucoside- toxins which not only taste bad, but interfere with digestion. To leach the acorn meal it was necessary to form a small pit in sand or other porous material. Continuous infusions with water filtered the acorn meal. This process could take several hours for completion. After leaching, the meal was made into bread or soup with the portion taken from the center of the pit being reserved for bread. The remaining meal, that which had adhered to the outside of the sand pit, was used for soup making. The grit settled to the bottom of the cooking basket to be discarded later.

The Indians at Anderson Marsh were not alone in relying on the acorn as a food staple. All tribes west of the mountain passes included acorns in their diet. The various tribes laid territorial claims to prime oak groves or certain prize acorn producing trees. A barter system was established, allowing the products not produced in one area to enhance the lives of those in another region. Obsidian and deerskin were exchanged for acorns in some regions. The Miwok Indians traversed the mountains to trade black oak acorns for pinon pine nuts of the Paiute at Mono Lake. Those from the Yuma tribe adjacent to the Colorado River traded gourds and their seeds for acorns from the Tipai tribe near San Diego.

Many California Indian tribes held ceremonies honoring the acorn harvest, or its imminent arrival. Some tribes sang acorn songs or held acorn dances, while others performed solemn rituals such as the dusting of funeral pyres with acorn meal to pay tribute to the deceased. For entertainment, acorn toys were crafted by many Indians, including acorn tops, whistles and games. Also, music helped celebrate the acorn. A Maidu acorn song from *Plants Used by the Indians of Mendocino County California,* by V.K. Chesnut went like this:

> The acorns come down from heaven.
> I plant the short acorns in the valley.

I plant the long acorns in the valley.
I sprout; I, the black acorn, sprout; I sprout.

The uses of oak were as diverse as the oaks of California. Oaks were an important source of medicines for the Indians. Medicines for bladder ailments were derived from oak teas. The bark was employed as both a medicine and dye. The dye was important in coloring fibers and roots for basket weaving, or to camouflage the fishnets so that they could blend in with the swirling and shadowy waters of creeks and lakebeds. Medicines vital to the tribe's health were derived from oak galls. The galls were also used by some tribes, such as the Lake Miwok Indians to produce an ink for their special blue-black tattoos. Like the acorn, the galls contain a lot of tannin which was pressed out of the malleable, young oak gall.

Oak galls are entomologically intriguing formations on oak trees, originating from wasp eggs. Galls range in size from two millimeters to grapefruit-size. Their shapes are assorted, as is the gall's coloration. They can be spherical, star-shaped, cup-like, tan, green, or a surprising hot-pink color! They are caused most often by miniature wasps from the family *Cynipidae* who lay their eggs on the oak tree. Once the wasp oviposits, the plant tissue swells, and a chemical process is stimulated by the oak or other host, causing a tumor, or gall to develop. The wasp may oviposit on leaves, buds, acorns, flowers, or roots. Even though the sizes and shapes of galls are so diversified, all galls are produced to protect and nourish the wasp larvae. Oak galls typically cause little or no harm to their hosts. The bulbous, tan puff-balls, pink stars, and other unusual-shaped objects stand out obtrusively against the leaves and branches of their unwitting hosts.

Oak galls aren't the only intruders who find oak limbs, bark, and leaves hospitable. Many epiphytic plants such as lichens, ferns, and fungi grow and thrive on oaks. An abundance of these plants proliferate up off of the woodland floor, preferring instead to nestle among the oak's strong limbs. Epiphytes dwell on oak bark where there is more light and more room to flourish. Luckily, the oaks are not harmed by all of this competition for residence on their bark. The gilled mushrooms living on oaks prosper by producing white or nearly invisible threads into the bark. Lichens are often found on the ground, tossed from their host after a storm. Some lichens are leafy, white, soft and flexible, while others, like the crustose lichen remain glued to the tree, a guano-like splotch contrasting sharply with the darker colored tree bark. Oaks throughout California and Anderson Marsh are draped with showy, exotic-looking *Ramalina menziesii*, or Spanish moss. In aboriginal times the pale-green pensile lichen was used for sanitary purposes, baby diapers, and also gathered for bedding.

Mistletoe is commonly found residing on oaks, but isn't always as friendly a guest as other oak residents. From the family Loranthaceae, mistletoe is usually quite harmless, but can damage the oak if the tree is already weak, or if too many plants take root in the tree's limbs. Mistletoe is known to many by the folklore surrounding it. It is, of course customary to get kissed when we stand under the mistletoe at Christmas time. European pre-Christian folklore promised that mistletoe had magical qualities, could cure sterility, and was thought of as an antidote to poisons. California Native Americans used mistletoe for medicinal purposes. Great care was needed when prescribing this plant, as there was the danger of causing sterility if not taken properly.

Mistletoe roosts high in the tree, taking full advantage of the plentiful light at the tree's crown. This aerial sprig-laden plant often gets its start high above the earth by an unwitting bird trying to wipe the sticky seeds off its feet onto the branches. Most seeds don't find a hospitable home, fall away, and dry up. But if a seed finds its way into a little niche in a twig, it soon takes root penetrating the bark and sucking water and minerals.

    Nature's methods of seed dispersal are multitudinous. While some plants produce seeds which are designed to float like parachutes to fertile ground, others are hitchhikers, adhering to animals for easy transport. Berry-producing plants have the advantage of having their seeds dispersed through bird droppings and other scat. Heat from fire is necessary for the knob-cone pine to shed its seeds. Seeds of some plants are capable of germinating for only mere days after being released from the parent plant, while others, like those from the oriental lotus remain viable for 3000 years.

The land throughout Anderson Marsh compels me to interpret each drifting sound and each print left on its soil. According to Henry David Thoreau, "The earth is not a mere fragment of dead history, stratum upon stratum like the leaves of a book, to be studied by geologists and antiquaries chiefly, but living poetry like the leaves of a tree, which precede flowers and fruit- not a fossil earth, but a living earth; compared with whose great central life all animal and vegetable life is merely parasitic. Its throes will heave our exuviae from their graves."

Marsh Trail

The morning is fresh and cloudless. To get to the Marsh Trail from the parking lot I follow the fenceline, then head south at the fence corner, moving west over the Ridge Trail through the oak woodland. The trail winds through what was once a reconstructed Pomo Indian village. As it once stood, the village site merged with its natural surroundings. Dried, golden tules were tied and arranged into dome-like shelters. According to Dr. John Parker, this area is believed to have been inhabited at least 14,000 years ago. I imagine what life was like here thousands of years ago. Anderson Marsh is a unique state park acquisition. It was built with the enduring flow of human encounter in mind, from prehistoric times to the present.

By studying clues from the past it is possible to construct a hypothesis about the settlement patterns as well as the former inhabitant's technology and population during each period of history. It was typical for a Native American family to have a hut which provided substantial shelter during winter and then served as the summer headquarters. During the summer, people made journeys to the coast for fish, salt, and other important staples. Another typical home was a temporary settlement on the nearby lakeshore or stream bank. It was characteristic for families from the village to move to huts in the mountains or hills for acorn gathering and deer hunting in the fall. Acorn gatherers had to move quickly, as the competition between squirrels, deer, and bear was stiff. It took about two weeks of steady gathering to ensure that the cache of acorns was substantive enough to provide acorn meal, mush, soup, and cakes for the year. The nutritional value of this staple is similar in content to whole wheat.

Along the leaf-strewn path I spot a ladybug on a fallen twig. I ponder the extent to which the incorporation of insects played in the diet of the Native Pomos. I know that grasshoppers played a small part in the California Indian's diet, but many more abundant and favored food stores prevailed. Grasshoppers were gathered by chasing them into cone-shaped pits while pounding the grass all about them. They were harvested by pushing a lit bundle of grass into the cone-hole. After collection, they were soaked in water for a time before they were baked in an earthen oven. The wings and legs were discarded after being broken, then winnowed off of the basket made for this purpose. Then, they could be consumed whole or cooked in a mush. Another method of harvesting grasshoppers was the building of a circular fire. When the fire reached the center, a nice pile of grasshoppers was both caught and roasted.

The ladybug takes flight, but as it lifts off, I find that other red beetles remain behind. Sue Hubbell quotes the great British biologist, J.B.S. Haldane in her book, *Broadsides From the Other Orders* as saying, "God has an inordinate fondness for beetles." Evidence has shown that there are more beetles on earth than virtually anything else in the animal kingdom, with about 370,000 species having been named so far.

There is an insect that played another part in the Pomo Indian life. That is Blue-Fly of Pomo mythology. According to S. A. Barrett, who doesn't specify the Pomo linguistic stock in which the story originates, the Gilaks, who are bird-like creatures, keep Blue-Fly as a slave to prepare Gilak's meals. This proves to be a difficult task, as Spider guards the gate called the Zenith Gate, which is the only means to get to the Upper World. The home of the Gilak contains four smoke holes along with a door which is placed on the south side, as is the custom of the Pomo houses. The Gilak's home has an added feature at the door, however, that of a deadly snare trap to catch unwelcome visitors.

The Pomo culture, like that of most indigenous peoples, was rich in mythology. Joseph Campbell, in *The Power of Myth,* said we tell stories to affirm our place in the world and to attune our lives with reality. He said, "Myths are clues to the spiritual potentialities of the human life." Of course most of us can't know how truly rich and rife with symbolism and connection to the life of the Native Americans the stories were. As in any translation, the textual meaning , nuance, cadence, and all of the minute details which make up a story tend to become distorted and diluted by changing the words from one culture to another. The Pomo had an oral tradition, therefore no written records were handed down generation to generation; rather, tribes listened to the elder's stories. The Southeastern Pomo language is the oldest of the original Pomo languages. All other dialects branched out from it.

California's first ethnographies were gleaned from recorded visits by Europeans to California's coasts. In reading documents such as the logs of Francis Drake in 1597 or Juan Cabrillo's voyages of 1542, descriptions, names of tribes, and folklore were found in garbled accounts. Also, the recordings of Franciscan missionaries led historians to form conclusions about California's past. As these accounts are all sketchy and slim, they are important when viewed together where they form a considerably more cohesive unit of ethnography. A few of the many, many myths we can read today are a result of the work of Dr. A.L. Kroeber. The late Professor Kroeber was associated with the University of California and was considered the premier anthropologist from the early twentieth century on. His exhaustive studies of California Indians summarized over 15 years of his work on everything from linguistics to social structures, demographics to religion. His work with the Yahi Indian, Ishi, described an unbelievably sad history. The true tale of Ishi's plight is that Ishi, a strong and wise Native Californian, became one of the last of his tribe after a group of settlers surrounded his village and killed his family in Tehama County in 1865. As history books are rewritten to include the accounts of both Native Americans and the military, too many "battles" as we once knew them, were, in reality outright massacres of Native Americans. Here I am speaking of Wounded Knee, South Dakota (1890), Bear River, Idaho (1863), Washita, Oklahoma (1868), and Bloody Island, California (1850).

I lived within walking distance to this mysterious and magical marsh for over seven years; and in this expansive county for forty-seven years. Every visit lays open the possibility of discoveries of the continuous creation all around me. The beauty of wildflowers playing host to fat bumblebees, succulent green life pushing its way from the earth below, or an elusive deer silently bounding off to places unknown to me.

Once I stumbled onto the scene of a former feast or slaughter, depending on whose side you happened to be on. The talon of a barn owl and puffs of white, downy feathers became evidence; noiseless clues from a clamorous night in the dirt and oak leaves. I still don't know to whom the barn owl fell victim. The eating habits of animals are almost as varied as the species themselves. A common method of many animals is to ingest their prey while it is still living. Other methods include biting their prey on the throat or drowning. Except for nature shows on television, we don't generally see animals falling victim to prey or dying of other natural causes. All of the life and death cycles are happening in startling quantities everywhere I walk, discretely hidden from view. Insects breeding and dying steadily, fungi and mosses proliferating and receding into the ecosystem. Naturalist Edwin Way Teale said, "In nature there is less death and destruction than death and transmutation." The paradoxes and dramas of the woodland play day and night, all for the price of a walk through its splendor. John Muir said,

> One is constantly reminded of the infinite lavishness and fertility of Nature-- inexhaustible abundance amid what seems enormous waste. And yet when we look into any of her operations that lie within reach of our minds, we learn that no particle of her material is wasted or worn out. It is eternally flowing from use to use, beauty to yet higher beauty, and we soon cease to lament waste and death, and rather rejoice and exult in the imperishable, unspendable wealth of the universe, and faithfully watch and wait the reappearance of everything that melts and fades and dies about us, feeling sure that its next appearance will be better and more beautiful than the last.

Continuing up the gentle slope, the trail leads me through a blue oak woodland. Interspersed with the oaks are the rich, brown hues of madrone and a variety of wildflowers. Once I *heard* the elegant, papery madrone bark peeling itself to reveal the glossy green trunk beneath. My friends, Allisun, Cathy, and their observant children brought that nuance of nature to my attention one hot summer day while walking this trail. The aristocratic wild iris thrives in this well-drained slope, as does blue-eyed grass, soaproot, and purple-colored clusters of brodiaea. Most of the plants growing here had an important purpose in the lives of the Pomos. Specialists in the tribe knew the value of each plant, be it nutritional or medicinal.

Imperceptibly underfoot are mice. Although I can't see them, I know they too, are residents of the complex web of life in the marsh. Some species of mice devise intricate highway systems to navigate their territories. Scientists estimate that in the space of one square mile of grassland there could be as many as 100 miles of mouse mazes. According to Edwin Way Teale, naturalist, there are around 100 different species of mouse, genus *Microtus*, in North America. Hardy and adaptable creatures, mice have carried on, despite their predators: bears, weasels, wildcats, foxes, skunks, hawks, and other birds of prey. Surprisingly enough, mice even have aquatic enemies. Mice are swimmers and can unwittingly end their days by being devoured by bass. Is this why mice are such prolific breeders?

I've hiked here just after a storm. The land is alive then; streams coursing down its back and sides are its veins. The countryside is being etched into a shape unlike ever before. Silently, but diligently, history is being made before my very eyes. I note the changes from the last time I passed through the canopy of oaks leading to the Marsh Trail. What was once a 10 foot oak trunk is now only a rotted, jagged stump. Millions of pieces of itself scattered about like a giant jigsaw puzzle lie waiting to complete this once lofty oak's lifecycle by nourishing the earth where it was born.

Everywhere I look is a study in Haiku. A stand of pines with the sun poking out from behind them. Boulders worn smooth and deep by unrelenting winter rains. A glossy, prickly pinecone. A lacey bit of moss tossed from its host by winds.

In rounding the bend where the motor-like sound of quail-wings-in-unison never fail to break into my thoughts, I'm surprised instead by a jackrabbit bolting past me. It came so close to me that, had I been as quick as it, and so desired, I could have reached out and touched its tawny fur.

The lull in the storm drew birds of all description out of their shelters. They were busy making home repairs and stocking up on easily caught fat bugs which had been washed out of hiding and stunned by the storm. They glided effortlessly between the bushes, navigating surprisingly small openings in the scrub with wings widespread. To master feats like this birds must keep their feathers dry, clean and perfectly arranged. They achieve this by constant preening of their 1,500-3,000 feathers. They're equipped with a preen gland under their tail which supplies preen oil, a natural water repellant. Just like housework, their work is never done.

The wind whips up an eddy of twirling leaves and deposits them to a new location. Stronger gusts smudge the sky a deep charcoal grey once again. I walk through an earthen green shag carpet. The most recent rains have caused further flooding throughout the county, but have also fashioned sparkling jeweled necklaces out of previously inconspicuous spider's homes.

The arachnid inhabitants, whose cousins in South America measure up to seven inches and feast on birds, are snugly hidden away. I carefully avoid stepping on one shimmering specimen.

The marsh swells and recedes about me. Rivulets of fresh fallen water play tic-tac-toe across the slope. I marvel at the underground architecture of a rodent, made evident by brown mounds of soil on the otherwise smooth greensward. I come upon a rocky slope covered with scrubby growth and interspersed with conifers and old oaks. The old oaks are silently and patiently undergoing the inevitable modification of a new season. "This year," I vowed to myself, "I'll witness the unfurling of tender new growth before the seemingly sudden transformation occurs." But I am too late. The show has started without me once again. It seems that each year I'm surprised by nature's "now you don't see it, now you do" act.

Responding to the lengthening days of spring is hard work for the oak. Billions of root hairs anchor and absorb dissolved minerals and transport them from cell to cell within the root, then defy gravity by nourishing a bud a lofty 30 feet or more away.

Beautiful lavender shooting stars dot my trail and lure me on. Blue and white hound's tongue, once used by Native Americans as a poultice for scalds and burns, entice me further. The grassy hill gradually changes to rock. Luxuriously soft lichen grow here. It can thrive in conditions as harsh as the Arctic Tundra.

Through taking a course on grasses given here at the state park by Greg de Nevers, resident biologist for Pepperwood Ranch in Santa Rosa, I've found that most of the grasses I'm seeing in the park are not native to this area. In the nineteenth century, when the state park was a working ranch, many

European grasses were introduced for grazing and for grain. The introduced varieties obliterated most native grasses. There is, however, a patch of purple needlegrass which graces this trail, a native which has managed to literally hold its ground over the years.

There are around 9,000 grass species in the world. Among the world's largest plant families, grasses rank fourth- following orchids, legumes, and composite flowers. As in times past, today grasses are an important food source for animals and people. Amazingly, grasses proliferate from above the Arctic Circle all the way down to the Antarctic continent. Grasses can be found in every habitat- desert, forest, prairies, tundra, savannas, and aquatic. Some species not only grow in still or running fresh or salt water, but on the surface of water as well, completely unattached to the ground. Grasses throughout the world range in size from only a few centimeters tall, like annual bluegrass, to over 100 meters high, as in giant bamboo.

In aboriginal times Eastern Pomo men played a grass game, or, *du we' qa'*. It was a guessing game involving the hiding of specially carved bones in handfuls of grass. Winners received magnesite cylinders, also known as Indian gold, or valuable clamshell beads.

Grass seed, or grain was harvested by Indians with specialty baskets that were woven by expert basket makers. Once the grain was ready for harvest, a large, woven utensil was used to strike the golden stalks of grain, while a circular, flat woven vessel was held underneath to catch the falling seed. The Lake County Museum in Lakeport, Schoolhouse Museum in Lower Lake, California Indian Museum and Cultural Center in Santa Rosa, California and the Grace Hudson Museum in nearby Mendocino County have many beautiful examples of Pomo Indian basketry.

Pomo Indian baskets are considered to be the most beautiful and unique baskets in the world, due to the intricacy of their twining and coiling techniques. Variations include lattice twining, open work, and methods incorporating both two and three-strand weaving. Traditionally, basket weavers could be men or women, but it was the men who most often produced durable fish traps and women who patiently prepared baskets used in special places, for ceremonies, for storage, cooking, and other routine work. Lucy McKay, related by marriage to renowned basketweaver, Mabel McKay, gave a basketweaving demonstration to my fourth grade students one day. At the time, Lucy's daughter Mary was a pupil of mine. Mary participates in the McKay basketweaving tradition. That day she joined her mother in a presentation of basketry techniques. They told of the preliminary preparation of the basket materials. The sedge roots, willow, redbud twigs, and bulrushes are gathered in the spring. Next, they are stripped of leaves and their bark coating with a sharp tool such as an obsidian flake. The approximately 20-inch strands are then coiled neatly and put away to cure (or dry). Once the materials are cured, for sometimes up to a year, the tools of the trade are brought out to work the bundle of woody fibers. An awl is used to separate the spaces in the roots to make a hole for a new strand, or warp rod. In times past, an awl was made from the leg-bone of a deer. Today, the appropriate tool with a sharp, steel point can be purchased from a hardware store. I will never forget what an honor it was to watch Lucy McKay teach us about weaving; creating and perpetuating history. She chose to affirm the identity of her people through a very beautiful tradition. The rich custom of Pomo basketweaving is summarized in Greg Sarris' book, *Mabel McKay: Weaving the Dream (Portraits of American Genius)* where he tells the fascinating story of the world-renowned Pomo basket weaver and medicine woman. She spent her life keeping alive her Pomo culture.

Now the trail descends to one that is narrower and lined with many beautiful specimens of andesite heaped haphazardly. These outcroppings are festooned with brightly colored lichens in shades of mustard yellow, gentle green, and poppy-colored orange. If I had chosen to bypass the Marsh Trail at the junction and continue west, I would have been led through the McVicar Trail, which was once owned by the National Audubon Society and managed by the local Redbud Audubon Society. Over 150 bird species have been logged there. In years of plentiful rains, the marsh swells, giving the mallards, American coots and western grebes a larger home. One morning I decided to explore the McVicar Trail. I was peripherally aware of foraging in the rushes. It was an American coot. According to my Audubon guidebook, coots are omnivores, feeding on snails, fish, worms, tadpoles, and vegetable matter. Coots nest either on a floating platform built entirely of aquatic vegetation or among the rushes in a reed nest. I stood stock-still, hoping not to disrupt its routine. I felt privileged to be allowed the pleasure of its company. The shady, willow-lined McVicar Trail leads to a picnic table, a perfect spot for viewing birdlife or enjoying refreshment before heading back to Anderson Marsh proper. I continue north along the Marsh Trail. Clear Lake spreads out in the northern distance.

Lake County's average annual rainfall is 21.6 inches. Out of this 21.6 inches, the county average is only one-half inch of rain in the months of June through September. This range in precipitation affects the level of Clear Lake by between 10 to 18 feet. The lake level then determines the amount and type of flora and fauna inhabiting its perimeter. The tules here provide a habitat for fish and mammals. Tules provide protection against erosion and improve the quality of the water with their natural filtration system. The Clear Lake of today has lost approximately 85 percent of its riparian vegetation. Those who live on the lake are encouraged to plant tules to improve habitat for fish and wildlife, as well as gain control of the blue-green algae blooms. Directions for planting tules may be provided by the County of Lake Water Resources.

It is believed that Clear Lake has always had algae, due to its relatively shallow waters. The lake is highly fertile in rich nitrogen, phosphorus, and iron which contribute to this growth. The algae in Clear Lake has certainly proliferated since aboriginal times. Modern-day gravel mining, and other development have caused streambeds to become destabilized and increased the flow of sediment into the lake. With the decrease in wetlands, the natural filtration process is hampered, adding to the growth of algae. A recent study, funded through a "Clean Lakes" grant from the Environmental Protection Agency determined that erosion is a major cause of algae growth in Clear Lake. With proper land management such as restoring creekbeds to eliminate erosion and the rehabilitation of wetlands, the problem could be lessened.

Fast growing hydrilla has recently invaded the lake. Hydrilla is an aquatic plant which, according to the Lake County Agricultural Commissioner and the California State Department of Food and Agriculture, grows an inch or more a day. If not controlled, it could make a matted mess and disrupt the water's ecology. The worst-case scenario would be if the plant worked its way through Cache Creek or other tributaries into the Central Valley.

Clear Lake, the largest natural lake within California's boundaries, attained its present size at least 400,000 years ago. The U.S. Geologic Survey has data that suggests that Clear Lake is the oldest living lake in the Western Hemisphere. Evidence points to formation of the lake during the Quaternary Period, a geologic time-division in the Cenozoic era, beginning around 1.6 million years ago and extending to the present time. For an understanding of the geological processes, it is just as John Muir wrote, "When we try to pick out anything by itself, we find it hitched to everything else in the universe." Although the science of geology concerns itself primarily with rocks and the earth's outer crust, geologists rely on other fields, like biology, chemistry, and physics in order to comprehend the earth's processes over time. Geologists believe that when the coastal mountain range formed, rising and separating, it was then that Clear Lake formed. Then, as now, the waters from the lake drained in an easterly direction. As time passed, the region's form changed, creating a drainage flow west to the Russian River. The U.S. Geological Survey reports that around 400 years ago a tectonic shift occurred in the lake basin causing a blockage to the Russian River. Natural resource specialists in the Department of Fish and Wildlife have detected the Sacramento perch in the Russian River, which they believe journeyed there at some point during the lake's changing outflows. Clear Lake's outflow redirected itself once again to the state's interior. It was then that the level of the lake began to rise up to 85 feet higher than it is now, to reach a new outlet, that of Cache Creek. Cache Creek forms Anderson Marsh's north and east borders and once drained into the Sacramento River. Due to crop irrigation by Yolo County, Cache Creek no longer reaches the Sacramento River. Throughout the tectonic shift that occurred, the lake outflow began to cut through Red Bank Gorge (the Cache Formation) which is located at the south end of the lake about one-half mile downstream from the State Highway 53 bridge. The lake outflow cut deeper and deeper through the Red Bank Gorge each year until it leveled off at the Grigsby Riffle, a solid rock formation.

As geological history goes, when the county's namesake, Clear Lake was formed it resulted in a highly mineralized zone. The Clear Lake basin is positioned in a graben, or depression between two faults, which is common in volcanic areas. Mt. Konocti, our lake's sentinel, is actually a volcanic composite cone which was built up of lava flows. Blatant evidence of the mineralized zone bubbles up in the form of a large soda spring at Soda Bay. Before Euro-Americans inhabited Lake County, mineral and hot springs which dot the county were used by Pomos. As Pomo legend has it, the hot springs in Clear Lake were formed by a despairing Indian named Princess Lupiyoma. There were also two giants, Kah-bel of Bartlett Mountain and Konocti. Kah-bel was in love with Konocti's daughter, Lupiyoma. Konocti was angry at this pronouncement and the two giants began to hurl boulders at one another across the water. A large rock struck Kah-bel with great force, killing him and sending his blood down the mountain. The stains are evident in the red color of Mt. Konocti even today. Konocti soon died of wounds sustained in the battle as well. The Princess' many tears which were spilled over the deaths of her loved ones formed Borax Lake, or Lake Hach-inhama. In her grief, she threw herself into Clear Lake or *Ka-ba-tin* and sank causing the bubbles to rise at Soda Bay.

Clear Lake is a rich fisherman's paradise today. Its 100 miles of shoreline and 70 square miles of surface water draws many water enthusiasts. Record-breaking bass are caught here in the shallow water during the spring spawning. Later in the summer they are said to be caught in deeper water. The lake's maximum depth is sixty feet. Catfish, black bass, and bluegills are other varieties successfully caught here. Interestingly, Clear Lake was once part of Mendocino County. The county boundaries were changed in 1852, when the Napa and Mendocino County line bisected the lake. The boundaries changed once again when Lake County was formed on May 20, 1861.

According to Lake County historian Henry K. Mauldin, Clear Lake was known as *Lupiyoma* and *Hok-has-ha*, as well as *Ka-ba-tin*. A lake creation story has it that there was once Frog and Badger. The badger asked Frog for a drink. Frog obliged. First he chewed a tree until it weakened, then toppled. Frog was then able to obtain the sap from the tree. He sucked the sap from the tree, then filled up a hollow in the ground with it. He allowed other frogs to help him, thereby creating Clear Lake.

Since marsh land is becoming increasingly rare, the State of California has recognized wetlands and riparian woodlands as two of the most important habitats needing protection. Marsh and wetland environments support lifeforms which rely solely on this particular habitat to survive. These areas are critical for fish and wildlife reproduction. The Rodman Slough and Ranch on the north shore of Clear Lake is one of the last remaining wetland marshes on Clear Lake, along with the shoreline of Big Valley. Being one of the largest watersheds in the Clear Lake basin, it is essential that this land be kept in public ownership. Thanks primarily to the unflagging efforts of Lakeport attorney Peter Windrem, Land Trust president Roberta Lyons, and the generous contributions of individuals, and state and federal agencies, The Lake County Land Trust has been successful in securing protection of close to 300 acres of this property, but there is more to be done. This scenic bioregion provides valuable wildlife habitat with its tules, wetlands, and oak-covered hills. It is an important stopover for migratory birds, and it is a great blue heron and osprey nesting site. Rodman Slough is a vital fish spawning area.

The tule marsh plays an important part in fish-feeding zones as well as feeding places for amphibians, waterfowl, and birds. The riparian woodlands play a vital part in the ecosystem, providing a habitat for the many insects, which are food sources for many animals. The other significant role it plays is its ability to provide nesting and roosting places, as well as cover for birds and animals. Other freshwater marshes in Northern California can be found in Laguna de Santa Rosa and Annadel State Park.

Anderson Marsh's past is rich almost beyond imagination. This extraordinary spot in California houses unique evidence of a previous culture. Here you can see what others saw long ago. The past is accessible now. It is this very accessibility to historic and prehistoric sites that has tempted some to obtain artifacts illegally. Many people do not realize that by disturbing or looting a site they are taking pieces of a puzzle; data which archaeologists need to investigate the past. By examining the fragile evidence of the past and sharing the information, we are given a chance to view our place in the continuum.

Archaeology is a multidisciplinary field, incorporating scientific methods and social sciences. As a sub-field of anthropology, archaeology reconstructs past lifeways and human behavioral patterns by studying artifacts and sites. Most native peoples of North America left no written records of their past, making the job of the archaeologist ever more important.

Any preconceived notions about archaeology and the

romance and excitement of it all were dispelled when I accompanied my brother David, who was an archaeologist, to a dig. Archaeology students from the University of California at Davis were conducting an excavation of a Patwin Indian site. When we arrived in the 85 degree heat of the late morning we were prepared to hike the five miles to the site. However, a student who was driving a supply truck offered us a ride. Gladly accepting, we hopped aboard the open bed just as the vehicle sped off. If I would have been wearing a hat I would have had to hold onto it. We flew around curves striking potholes, rocks, and other road perils. The bushes, which were scraping the truck, became a blur of various hues of green. Behind us great brown clouds of dust lingered to mark our path. After the wild ride we brushed ourselves off and embarked on a rubber raft across Cache Creek. The fertile, wet smell of the shady creek was intoxicating.

    The raft was attached to a rope with a pulley system and we pulled ourselves across the creek, our wake dispersing the languorous meeting place of a half-dozen fat carp. We were duly warned about the four-foot rattlesnake spotted in the bushes where we were to disembark. This was rather Indiana Jonesesque so far, I thought. Wild rides, snakes- what next? The romance ended at the trail's conclusion. Archaeology is tedious, painstaking work! Everywhere I looked student archaeologists were digging in the hard soil with shovels, picks, and trowels. Soil samples were meticulously sifted through screens, dust flying, heat rising. Holes in the earth were carefully measured and mapped; and artifacts were precisely tagged, to be cataloged in complete detail by computer later.

    Archaeological research methods were first found to be of great value culturally around 1890, but became a more common means of gaining information in 1937, with the work of

A.L. Kroeber and Julian Steward. Today, as the modern world encroaches on the land, archaeology is a vital, extremely necessary science.

The past comes alive through the science of archaeology. It has been determined that tribal territory of the Pomo Indians is bordered by the Cahto and Yuki tribes to the north and northeast, the Patwin to the east, Lake Miwok and Wapppo to the south, and Coast Miwok to the west. The area of the Pomo encompassed much of what is now Lake, southern Mendocino and Sonoma counties, as well as a small area in Glenn County. Actually, the Pomos are a people comprised of many bands with similar languages. The complex, rich languages are divided into so many dialects that a Southern Pomo would have as much trouble understanding an eastern Pomo as a French-speaking person would have trouble understanding a Dutch-speaking person. The Pomoan languages have at least one thing in common, that is their system of five vowels with an involved set of consonants. The name "Pomo" has several meanings. It means "those who live at or reside in a group or place," "at red earth hole" or, "magnesite hole."

Several acorn granaries, time's signals, dot the Marsh Trail. The tree stumps, grey ghosts of the trees that they once were, are now laced with holes that have been meticulously filled with acorns by productive acorn woodpeckers. By storing their cache in this manner, the acorn woodpeckers can return later to a feast of acorns, and probably insects which have found the food attractive too. Other acorn-eaters are not equipped, as the acorn woodpecker is with his specially-shaped bill, to extract the snugly fitting acorns.

Another woodpecker, the red-headed woodpecker is

featured in the Pomo Indian Myth, "Owl Tricks Coyote." It seems that Coyote went far up into the mountains where he met Owl, who was well-known for his gift of singing during the night. Coyote was curious about Owl's ability, so he asked just how it was that he was able to make that noise at night. Owl told Coyote that he simply found a hole in a tree, crawled inside, then stuck his head out and was able to sing out loud. Coyote thought that sounded easy enough, so he tried it. He found a hole in a tree, and tried to crawl inside to stick out his head, but he got stuck. He died in the tree. A red-headed woodpecker happened along one day, and began pecking the tree. His diligent pecking made a hole in the tree, and he found Coyote's bones. He had just tossed the bones to the ground, when Blue Jay came by and sang his song, bringing Coyote back to life. Coyote, disgruntled at being disturbed, snarled at Blue Jay, saying, "You are always in the way when I am trying to sleep," then went on his way.

As I rest under the shade of an oak tree on the Marsh Trail, I wonder how it is possible for the trees to establish themselves while growing in such close proximity to the saturated marshlands. The rock-strewn land obviously provides for sufficient drainage, while the nutrient-laden soils feed the trees. While overlooking the heaving hills I'm reminded that for the people of ancient times this land was known so thoroughly that a single rock or tree may have borne a name. The land was rich with meaning for those living so intimately with their surroundings. Bill Moyers addresses Mary Catherine Bateson, anthropologist, during an interview in *A World of Ideas: Conversations with Thoughtful Men and Women about American Life Today and the Ideas Shaping our Future*. He said, "What we name something makes a difference. You point out that if you think of a tree more like a woman, than as a post, you're going to be thinking differently about how to treat a tree. That applies to what you think about the earth, what you think about a family, and what you think about every object and person in your embrace."

Indentations and striations found on some of the special rocks here at Anderson Marsh indicate human use over time. The workings (called petroglyphs) found here keep their true purpose concealed within the beautiful symbols incised on stone. Educated guesses as to the meaning of certain cupules which were carved or worn into the boulders include women's fertility and religious ceremonies. I respect the sacred aura of my surroundings. Some things will and should remain mysteries.

Ancient rock art is found throughout the world. The discovery of the cave art of the Cro-Magnons near the French town of Vallon-Pont-d'Arc, in the Rhone Alps region brought to light exquisite paintings (called pictographs) of a variety of animals. The wooly rhinoceroses were in a prominent area of display, set amongst other carnivores such as bears and lions. From data recovered during archeological excavations, it is known that between 20,000 to 18,000 years ago (roughly the time of the French cave paintings) that reindeer was a staple in the Paleolithic menu. Scientists were surprised that cave paintings found in the *Grotte Chauvet* didn't feature more reindeer. Discoveries like these bring up more questions than answers. I'm sure there is speculation as to why the art doesn't depict humans, insects, stars, or other aspects prevalent in the lives of Cro-Magnon. No culture spent every waking minute securing sustenance or on industrial work. Certainly esthetic pleasures were enjoyable pastimes of every culture. Dancing, singing, sculpture, and painting are all human activities felt to be immensely satisfying.

You are an archaeologist. You're studying designs found on the walls of the rough caves of California's coast range. You're in Southern Valley Yokut territory. Centuries swirl past as you imagine the routines of a peaceful tribe. The pungent smell of the cook fire mingles with the perfume of the surrounding pine and oak trees. Everyone has a place in this society, be it medicine man, mid-wife, shaman, or basket weaver. The family is grouped by patrilineal totems. The totem is a symbol taken from nature: an animal, plant, landscape feature, or other natural phenomenon. A father's totem symbol is passed on to all of his children. The totem was regarded as sacred, therefore the animal which one prayed to was never hunted and eaten, be it an eagle, raven, or antelope totem. Music is being played with a wood whistle, flute, a stick, or bone rattle and musical bow. You are humbled at the honor of witnessing the creation of a song.

According to *The Handbook of North American Indians Volume 8* published by The Smithsonian Institution, it was the Chumash Indians who left some of the most beautiful and fascinating rock art in all of the United States. Evidence of an intricate concentric circle design is found in the Painted Cave of San Marcos Pass, outside of Santa Barbara, California. These paintings are presumed to have been connected with girl's puberty rites. Out of 58 counties in California, at least 39 are known to have occurrences of rock art. The characteristics of the art were studied extensively and nine main styles have been identified. Examples in the Great Basin area show big-horn sheep, bows, and arrows. The northeast petroglyph motif depicts red, black, yellow, and blue geometric designs, while some southwest coast petroglyphs feature stick figures and other designs.

Of course we can never know for sure the reason and meaning behind any given art. Thousands of years after the creation of rock art, artists of a different genre emerged. Scholars today wonder at the form and content of works by Claude Monet, or Georgia O'Keeffe. Celebrating color and form have been and, it appears, always will be central to mythological, religious, historical, or literary events.

Once, many years ago I stood in the Louvre Museum in Paris among the great works of art. A melange of feelings rushed over me while I breathed the rarified air of so many examples of human endeavor. Ideas flowed and swirled through the building, right off the canvasses and statues in a mixture so heady it took my breath away. Works by Botticelli and Tintoretto were evocative of a Schumann piano concerto, while other paintings by Rembrandt and Vermeer conveyed a magisterial impression and were locked into the complex forces that shaped their times. If those same artists were commissioned to paint during the present, what would those pictures look like? Have we really learned anything from history? I was at the fountainhead of such a vast array of ideas and representations of the world that I was awestruck. I was left with a peaceful, solemn reverence as though in a cathedral, or among a giant stand of redwoods, or among the mysterious Pomo petroglyphs.

In the not too distant past, Native Americans were often featured in books and movies as crude savages. This same notion helped justify early European-American conquest. Although the Pomo material culture could appear sparse by modern standards, they were in fact the owners of a diverse and interesting society. Drawing on their surroundings they devised games, dances, ceremonies, and art. How many people do you know today who have such an intimate and thorough knowledge of their environment? Chief Seattle said:

> You must teach your children that the ground beneath their feet is the ashes of your grandfathers. So that they will respect the land, tell your children that the earth is rich with the lives of our kin. Teach your children what we have taught our children, that the earth is our mother. Whatever befalls the earth befalls the sons of the earth. If men spit upon the ground, they spit upon themselves.

Springtime was the season when women and children gathered plant foods, while the men hunted or fished. Common edible food resources for the Pomo in spring included greens such as cowparsnip, miner's lettuce, hedge mustard, and angelica greens. The young green tops of lupines were collected and eaten, as was clover, dandelion, and fireweed.

Another valuable plant was the tule. It was not only an important food item, but served many other important purposes as well. It was used to make huts, shoes, boats, mantles (or capes), leggings, and mats for food and seating. It was also shredded and used for baby diapers.

Many varieties of bulbs were utilized in the Pomo culture. Some were prepared by baking or roasting, then eaten. The soap plant bulb had another purpose, however. As its name implies it was used as soap for washing purposes. It was also used as a poison to stun fish for easy catching by first pounding the root, then throwing it into the lake at a pre-determined fishing spot. The land around Clear Lake was fruitful and provided abundantly for Native Americans. Bracken ferns were eaten by namesake, Galileo Galilei, observed that the small satellites, Io, Europa, Callisto, and Ganymede orbited Jupiter. He published these findings in a book called, *The Starry Messenger* in 1610, thereby sending shock-waves through the Vatican.

In California's society today we're learning the meaning of moderation and balance- lessons we could learn from aboriginal cultures. As in Wendell Berry's poem, "What We Need is Here" in his book, *Home Economics*, we have to learn from both the "technocrats" who espouse an "Industrial Paradise" and the "nature romantics" who promise Eden. Extremes of one form or the other aren't feasible, but harmony with wilderness is possible, as evidence from the past points out in its many stories, if we but care to listen.

know today who have such an intimate and thorough knowledge of their environment? Chief Seattle said:

> You must teach your children that the ground beneath their feet is the ashes of your grandfathers. So that they will respect the land, tell your children that the earth is rich with the lives of our kin. Teach your children what we have taught our children, that the earth is our mother. Whatever befalls the earth befalls the sons of the earth. If men spit upon the ground, they spit upon themselves.

Springtime was the season when women and children gathered plant foods, while the men hunted or fished. Common edible food resources for the Pomo in spring included greens such as cowparsnip, miner's lettuce, hedge mustard, and angelica greens. The young green tops of lupines were collected and eaten, as was clover, dandelion, and fireweed.

Another valuable plant was the tule. It was not only an important food item, but served many other important purposes as well. It was used to make huts, shoes, boats, mantles (or capes), leggings, and mats for food and seating. It was also shredded and used for baby diapers.

Many varieties of bulbs were utilized in the Pomo culture. Some were prepared by baking or roasting, then eaten. The soap plant bulb had another purpose, however. As its name implies it was used as soap for washing purposes. It was also used as a poison to stun fish for easy catching by first pounding the root, then throwing it into the lake at a pre-determined fishing spot. The land around Clear Lake was fruitful and provided abundantly for Native Americans. Bracken ferns were eaten by roasting or boiling the immature curled tops. Their roots were also a source of food and were prepared by boiling.

Berries were an abundant food source. Manzanita, wild grape, gooseberry, salmon berry, and blackberries were some of the berries available in this area.

In addition to all of the foods aforementioned, there was plentiful game: elk, deer, rabbit, fish and fowl, as well as seafood. Trips to the coast brought abalone, surf fish, and seaweed for the food-stores. Shells for bead-making were brought back as well.

With my notebook on my lap, I sketch the andesite rock outcropping which lines the other side of the trail. I'm no artist, but I find that by making an attempt to bridge art and nature I can discover more about the environment. I use a number two pencil to jot down notes describing the display of colorful lichen growing on the rock- some yellow, orange, and soft green. NASA Mars scientist Dr. Chris McKay has studied algae and lichen in the frigid, ice-covered lakes of the Antarctic. He considers this as an analog to the cold conditions on Mars. The average temperature in Antarctica is -20 degrees C (-5 degrees F), which proves to be the most Mars-like place on earth, motivating NASA to study this region in more depth. The controversy over the exciting proposal that a meteorite, labeled ALH84001, discovered in the Allen Hills ice field in Antarctica in 1984, could contain fossilized life forms from Mars is on-going. While scientists debate whether the microstructures are biological or mineral in nature, the public's imagination soars along with NASA's "cheaper, faster" launches to Mars.

What would NASA scientists make of the lichen specimens here at Anderson Marsh? Other scientists exploring the miniature worlds encased in ancient Antarctic ice have also found a variety of lifeforms from among algae, fungi, bacteria, and a few diatoms. Some forms with admittedly strange shapes have recently been discovered- and named: Mickey Mouse and Klingon are the names given to a colony of fluffy microbes buried for thousands of years in the Antarctic ice and studied by Richard Hoover of NASA's Marshall Space Flight Center and Dr. S.S. Abyzov of the Russian Academy of Sciences. Their work of identifying items found in the ice is tedious and time-consuming. But past studies of deep ice core samples from the Vostok Station, about 620 miles (1,000 km) from the South Pole have shown that the microorganisms freeze, then go into an anabiotic state; alive but inactive "like suspended animation." Scientists have been successful in reviving and culturing anabiotic bacteria, yeast, and fungi from the ice cores.

    Diane Ackerman in *A Natural History of the Senses* says, "We can extend our senses with the help of microscope, stethoscope, robot, satellite, hearing aid, eyeglasses, and such, but what is beyond our senses we cannot know." New data in from NASA's Jupiter Galileo Project Mission is helping to define what is beyond, and previously unknown. This amazing mission was started in 1989 when the Galileo Orbiter and Probe were launched from Space Shuttle Atlantis. This fascinating mission took a tour of our solar system's largest planet, Jupiter, orbited four of its moons, and studied its immense magnetosphere. After its six year voyage to Jupiter, Galileo launched a probe into Jupiter's atmosphere, which is comprised mainly of hydrogen and helium. The mission went into a two year extension; the GEM's or Galileo at Europa Mission. Europa is one of Jupiter's sixteen known moons. Scientists believe that Europa contains an ocean beneath its icy surface- making it one of two oceans, ours being the other, in our solar system. In 1609, the project's namesake, Galileo Galilei, observed that the small satellites, Io, Europa, Callisto, and Ganymede orbited Jupiter. He published these findings in a book called, *The Starry Messenger* in 1610, thereby sending shock-waves through the Vatican.

In California's society today we're learning the meaning of moderation and balance- lessons we could learn from aboriginal cultures. As in Wendell Berry's poem, "What We Need is Here" in his book, *Home Economics*, we have to learn from both the "technocrats" who espouse an "Industrial Paradise" and the "nature romantics" who promise Eden. Extremes of one form or the other aren't feasible, but harmony with wilderness is possible, as evidence from the past points out in its many stories, if we but care to listen.

Anderson Flats Trail

The rain rapidly advanced and then retreated, leaving only untidy shreds of fluff in the skies above Anderson Marsh. Cloud shadows ran like deer over the grasslands. Weather is no doubt, one of the leading topics of conversation the world over. Weather has played key roles in inestimable events. Everything from moods to wars can be attributed to the weather of a given day. When the Japanese fought to keep the Mongols from landing on the shores of Japan in the thirteenth century, weather certainly intervened. A typhoon blasted the Mongolian fleet and ended their assault. Since then, the Japanese have called typhoons the Divine Wind, or *Kamikaze*.

Some doctors believe changes in the weather cause people under emotional stress to act erratically. Similarly, extremes of temperature cause crime rates to soar, and even suicides have been attributed to the weather. Political unrest occurs more often during the heat spells of summer than at any other time during the year. For example, the French Revolution began in July. Scientists believe ions, electrically charged particles of matter all about us in the atmosphere, are the key to the effect weather has upon us. Some of us probably know a person who can predict a storm by a headache that is caused, some scientists say, by an overload of positive ions which consist partially of carbon dioxide.

Weather unquestionably played a part in the settlement of the west. Men and women drove wagons and walked day after day in all kinds of weather. Many died in the burning heat, rainstorms, or freezing weather along the way.

Lake County boasts an average temperature of 70 degrees. Today isn't quite so moderate, however, with the thermometer reading 47 degrees.

On a day like this, when the dirt along the Anderson Flats Trail is sufficiently moist, one may discern the myriad comings and goings of woodland creatures- too much rain and the footprints would have been obliterated. I can easily tell the hastily-left quail's marks. The tracks of a deer are identifiable to me. In consulting Harper and Row's *Complete Field Guide* I can identify skunk prints. I wonder if I've passed its burrow? Being nocturnal hunters, any skunk seen about during daylight hours should be reported to animal control, as rabies would be suspect.

I enjoy the matinee on the marsh. Nature's show this afternoon includes thick, extravagant thunder clouds contrasted by a powder blue sky. Turkey vultures lazily glide in the foreground. They have a wingspan of six feet and are carrion-eaters. The presence of vultures and other scavengers aesthetically assist nature by cleaning up the environment. Vultures have bare, ugly heads and big feet. Okay, so you don't have to look good to perform a necessary service in nature! Their big feet help them to hold onto carcasses. Nature has also equipped them with a strong beak for tearing prey, as well as keen eyesight and a well-developed sense of smell.

The mass of condensed water in the sky beyond the birds

offers an infinite variety of shapes to observe. The isolated puff I pick out from the other formations is a heap of beauty- it looks like a magnificent cauliflower in the sky! Clouds generally form in earth's troposphere, ranging in height from the ground to 37,000 feet. Clouds help meteorologists forecast the weather. Clouds can be classified in three ranges: high clouds are 16,500 feet to 45,000, middle-range clouds are 6,500 feet to 23,000, and low cloud cover ranges from zero to 6500 feet. Classifying clouds including cirrus, altocumulus, stratocumulus, etc. began in 1803. This was an international classification based on the shape, structure, and texture of clouds and is used in revised form today.

The Anderson Flats Trail greets me with a swelling wind. Prolonged gusts brush my cheek like velvet. The valley spreads out before me, metamorphosing into oak woodlands to the south and west. Emerald hues of the wetlands create a contrasting landscape to the north side. The balletic grace of the willow trees draw the eye toward Cache Creek.

If I close my eyes I can envision one of the first European-American families to settle here: John Melchisadeck Grigsby, his wife Margaret, and their 10 children. They built and occupied the original, central portion of the ranch house. (I wonder how they all fit into that small abode?) Life on the ranch was rich in many ways. The indescribably clear air of Lake County, the quiet and peace of the balmy valley- so quiet that you could almost hear the tule reeds growing, and the cheerful monologue of a meadowlark were certainly among the riches. The rewards of the sights and sounds of the graceful valley were balanced by the hard work that ranch life entailed. Their food and shelter needed to be provided for, and clothes had to be made. An annual sojourn to Napa City with an ox team via Pope Valley, albeit a difficult and tedious trip, must have been a welcome diversion from pitching hay, cleaning corrals, and performing other chores at the ranch. The juxtaposition of clean, clear views, the smell of new-mown hay, and fragrant fields of wildflowers competing with the noise of the wagon wheels and the dust they stirred was ever-present.

According to a story told to Henry Mauldin, late Lake County Historian, "Mels" Grigsby, as John Melchisadeck Grigsby was known, was not a handsome man. Mauldin tells the following story regarding this fact:

> A boy from San Francisco came up to see an uncle of his in Lower Lake. He had never seen this relation nor did he know just where he lived. Grigsby was in Lower Lake on this special day and this boy approached him and called him Uncle So and So. Grigsby denied the relationship and the name. The boy insisted. Finally Grigsby wanted to know why the boy was so sure. The boy then said that the only description and instructions his folks had given him before leaving was to go to Lower Lake and when he seen the ugliest man he ever seen in his life, that would be his uncle. The boy said, 'Your['re] it'.

When the Grigsbys acquired the ranch now known as Anderson Marsh, the region was called Hot Springs Township and was part of Napa County. This area was appointed as part of Lake County's jurisdiction in 1861 by an act of the state legislature.

The Grigsbys of Anderson Marsh were involved in the

controversial Cache Creek dam incident. In 1866, a San Francisco-based water company, the Clear Lake Water Works Company, erected a dam across Cache Creek. The dam caused the waters in Clear Lake to rise 13 feet over normal and flooded thousands of acres of prime farmland in the county. Many, many people were adversely affected by the construction of the dam. Among those affected by the flooding were the Grigsbys. After two extremely rainy years, the Grigsbys and others owning property repeatedly flooded by the dam brought suit against the water company. Some of the lawsuits were settled out of court or dropped, but none were prosecuted to judgment. Grigsby won the original case, but later the California State Supreme Court rescinded the decision on a technicality.

The dam housed a large flour mill, and plans for its future included a wool mill and the transportation of Clear Lake waters to San Francisco. On October 14, 1868, 300 armed vigilantes came to Cache Creek seeking justice for the flooding of their fertile agricultural lands and homes. The disgruntled residents disassembled the millworks, and, piece by piece took apart the dam. They went about their jobs in an orderly, almost methodical manner, not even allowing so much as a sip of liquor within the work area. One old-timer named "Pap" Way tried to smuggle a bottle of whiskey in by stashing it in the lining of his pants. His secret was soon found out, and the whiskey was "poured upon the ground in his very thirsty presence." During this time messages were sent and intercepted by "Uncle George Tucker," who was dispatched to Guenoc. At that time, Guenoc was a small town in Coyote Valley along the way to Calistoga. While some of the men were taking down the dam with block and tackle, another body of organized men held the superintendent of the water company, county officers, and the sheriff at bay. One of the men being held, Sarshel Bynum, the County Clerk, wasn't going to stand for the outrageous situation, so he made an attempt to move off the wagon full of officials. The book entitled *History of Lake County 1881* recalls how Sarshel Bynum was deterred by an old hunter named Mr. Welty:

> Mr. Welty was upwards of eighty at that time, and as gray as a badger. He was very diminutive in stature, and had a very long-barreled gun- one of the old-fashioned muzzle-loading flint-locks that were common a century or more ago. Mr. Bynum proceeded to make good his words, that he 'would not stand it any longer', and started to move off. Old Mountaineer was not to be trifled with in that manner; so, backing off till he could get the entire length of his gun barrel in a horizontal between him and Mr. Bynum, he leveled his old piece on him, and shouted out in stentorian tones: 'STAND, *Sarshel*, I say, STAND!' And Sarshel stood. For many years that was a 'catch phrase' all over the county, but it was always very repulsive to Mr. Bynum's ears, although he was forced to hear it very often in after years.

The Cache Creek dam buildings were mysteriously destroyed by fire later that same night. As a result of the damages, the water company brought suit against the County of Lake for $200,000. Tragically, The Clear Lake Water Works bought the Grigsby ranch in 1870, forcing the Grigsby family to move on.

The Cache Creek Dam may no longer exist, but problems revolving around today's Clear Lake Dam, built in 1915 by the Yolo County Flood Control and Water Conservation District incite criticism and complaints from shoreline residents. The dam releases up to 21,000 cubic feet of water per second, but the five mile channel running from Clear Lake to the dam includes a naturally occurring rock barrier called the Grigsby Riffle. This gives the channel a limited capacity of just 2,500 cubic feet per second. Critics of the dam's control have concluded, through their own observation, that problems with the Grigsby Riffle could be alleviated by opening the dam's floodgates sooner. Clear Lake Dam officials claim that opening the gates sooner is not the answer. The officials add that the gates would only become clogged with debris if opened sooner. To complicate matters further, Yolo County and Lake County have fought in court over this dam throughout the years. For example, in 1920 a decree by the lakeshore resort owners was set forth directing dam officials to keep Clear Lake at a level between zero and 7.56 feet on the Rumsey Gauge, a special device made to measure Clear Lake's level. This was done to maintain high recreational lake levels. To meet the rules of the decree the lake may rise between 7.56 and 9 feet at flood stage for up to 10 consecutive days. The Rumsey Gauge is kept under careful watch.

In 1940 another decree was issued which prohibits the expansion of the Grigsby Riffle area. The area around the Grigsby Riffle was expanded in the 1930s to allow for heavier water flow, and caused soil erosion to landowners downstream due to the increased flow.

The U.S. Army Corps of Engineers recommended enlarging the outflow channel to increase the dam's output in 1983, but fortunately for the sensitive Anderson Marsh wetlands area, the idea ran into opposition by environmentalists. John Parker was foremost in highlighting the negative environmental impacts of this project. After Parker pointed out that the costs outweighed the benefits, the federal government tabled the project.

John Melchisadeck Grigsby's uncle, Captain John Grigsby, rode out to California with a party of 100 wagons from Missouri in the spring of 1845. Among the adventurers in this party was William B. Ide, the soon-to-be first and only President of California. Ide, teacher and carpenter, kept a journal of the historic events later known as the Bear Flag Revolt of 1846. Among the 33 men who played a part in the revolt against Mexican authority and the short-lived Republic of California was Captain John Grigsby. The turn of events was precipitated by a statement issued from General Jose Don Castro. Castro stated that American settlers were not welcome in California and that their land was to be confiscated. Because Ide had just made the arduous trip west about a year earlier and was settled in the Sacramento River Valley on a large ranch with his wife and family, he felt that he had something worth fighting for. Ide and 32 others (John Grigsby included), rode to Sonoma, the capitol of the northern section of California where General Mariano Vallejo lived. Vallejo, the son of an important Californio family, maintained the military garrison in Sonoma. Several years earlier, the Mexican government had sent him to Sonoma with instructions to establish a pueblo to dissuade the Russians from colonizing *La Frontera del Norte*, or the area north of San Francisco. During that time, Vallejo sent his vaqueros to Clear Lake to round up Southeastern Pomo to work as slave labor on his ranch near Sonoma. On one of these trips his men burned most of an Indian village as they gathered in their ceremonial building.

Then, on June 14, 1846 the 33 Bear Flaggers drew lots to see who would enter Vallejo's home and demand his surrender. Grigsby was elected captain, and along with several other men demanded to see the general. No one in the party could speak much Spanish, but Vallejo understood what the men were there for through their gestures and what little Spanish they could articulate. After a while, the men who stayed outside became curious about what was taking place inside. William B. Ide was sent inside and reported (from *William B. Ide* by George Kirov):

> The general's generous spirit gave proof of his usual hospitality as the richest wines and brandies sparkled in the glasses, and those who had thus unceremoniously met soon became merry companions, more especially merry visitors. There sat Mr. Semple, just modifying a long string of articles of capitulation; there sat Merritt, his head fallen; there sat Knight, no longer able to interpret, and there sat the newly made captain, as mute as the seat he sat upon. The bottles had well nigh vanquished the captors.

After much brandy and wine were consumed, the army of homesteaders could report to Lieutenant John C. Fremont that their mission was a success. The Bear Flag was hoisted in the Sonoma Plaza and Mexico ceded California to the United States.

The Anderson Flats Trail is seeped in history. If the valley oak standing in the center of the field could talk, what lessons we could reap. This oak is known as the Kite Tree, as it is frequented by black-shouldered kites. These uncommon masters of the sky are declining in population in North America. They're easy to recognize as they beat the air: They hover like a toy kite while hunting. Kites and other birds have many hollow bones-this keeps their weight low and assists in flight. The bird's air sacs and lack of teeth also factor in to the bird's ability to fly. Interestingly, birds today descended from the Archaeopteryx: small dinosaurs which were about the size of a pigeon, from the Triassic period. The Archaeopteryx appeared as a cross between a dinosaur and a bird. When today's black-shouldered kites have sighted their prey they descend feet first to grasp it and then take to the skies. Their diet consists of insects, birds, field mice, or other small mammals.

I've been fortunate enough to observe a representative from another bird order flapping and gliding over Clear Lake: The white pelican. From the order, Pelecaniformes, the white pelican has a wingspan that may reach 10 feet, and may weigh up to 33 pounds. Pelicans put their great pouches to use when they fish in the lake. They can hold fish in their pouches to dine on at a later time, or to feed their offspring. I would love to see their nests which resemble the crude structures built by the herons. Typically, white pelicans breed throughout the western United States and Canada, migrating to Florida for the winter.

Animal migration (the periodic movements of animals due to seasonal changes) usually occurs before or after the breeding season. About half of the 8,580 known bird species in the world migrate. The world record for distance migrated has to go to the Arctic tern, who flies each fall from the Arctic Circle to the world down under, the Antarctic Ocean- over 22,000 miles. Many bats travel seasonally to lands with warmer weather, as do butterflies and fish. After the animal has responded to the built-in "trigger" to exit one territory for another, zoologists believe there are many components which may influence the path it takes on its migratory journey. Birds appear to navigate by the celestial signs of the stars and sun and may even be sensitive to earth's magnetic field and to the rotation on its axis.

Another example of nature's homing device is found in fish: Fish can detect the chemical odors remaining in rivers from their forebears during times long forgotten.

A pale crescent moon reveals itself in the skies above Anderson Marsh. Its main "seas," (or *Mares* as they are called in Latin) remain in shadow- the Mares Imbrium, Fecundatis, Chrisium, Serenitatis, and Tranquillitatis. Before the 16th century it was common belief that our earth was the center of the universe. How far, literally, we have come. Gazing at the moon over the marsh, I wonder, what does it feel like to tread upon our only natural satellite which has but one-sixth of earth's gravity? Only a few incredibly brave Americans can say for sure. Lunar Prospector, the diminutive, low budget craft orbiting the moon, discovered 10 to 300 million tons of water ice at the lunar poles with its Neutron Spectrometer. Can a lunar base colony be far behind?

Through NASA I became Lunar Certified- a distinction which enabled me to borrow one of America's national treasures, the moon rocks. Likewise, my fourth and fifth grade students became lunar experts and docents of the moon; in turn teaching hundreds of students, one classroom at a time, about these unique specimens. Rocks from the moon are similar to our own terrestrial rock; however, there are notable differences. For instance, by analyzing their chemistry, scientists have found that the specimens brought back from the Apollo Missions contain no water, while many rocks on earth retain at least a percentage or two. Moon rocks formed about four and a half billion years ago where there was almost no free oxygen. Some of the iron contained in lunar rocks was not oxidized when the lunar lavas formed and is still present in the form of small crystals of metallic iron; hence, the rocks could "rust" if they came in contact with the earth's atmosphere.

The samples we observed in my classroom were actually museum mounted in a disc of plastic. Microscopic inspection shows that moon rocks are made of the same chemical elements that make up earth rocks, but in different proportions. They contain more of the common elements calcium, aluminum, and titanium than most earth rocks do. Moon rocks contain rare elements, like hafnium and zirconium. Also, moon rocks are richer in high-temperature elements and poorer in low-temperature elements, leading scientists to believe that the material forming the moon was once heated to much higher temperatures than material which formed the earth.

Another interesting fact is that the chemical composition of the moon is different in different places. The light regions of the moon which we see are the Highlands. As their name implies, the Highlands are higher, more rugged, and made of several different kinds of rock which cooled slowly, deep within the moon. The darker regions of the moon (which in combination give us the "man in the moon") are called "maria" and these are low, level areas covered with layers of basalt lava. All moon rocks are igneous; meaning they were formed by the cooling of molten lava.

No sedimentary rocks (like limestone or shale which are deposited in water) have ever been found on the moon. The moon's mottled surface is made up of craters which were formed by catastrophic asteroid bombardment that died away about four billion years ago. Then, for the next half billion years great floods of lava rose from inside the moon and poured out over its surface, filling in the large impact basins to form the dark parts of the moon that we now see. Back in the classroom we were in awe when we held six of the samples collected by NASA astronauts from the stark surface of the moon: Highland Soil, Mare Soil, Breccia, Orange Soil, Anorthosite, and Basalt.

The Anderson Flats Trail exhibits a vertisol soil condition: The countless cracks and crevices are the result of the shrink-swell "behavior" of clay soils throughout the repeated dry heat of summer and cool damp of winter. Bees, lizards, and a multitude of insects seek out the cool, dark enclaves of this trail. A tiny black, shiny object lying on the trail winks in the sunlight; it is an edge-modified flake of obsidian. I examine it closely with a handlens, trying to imagine who held this artifact long before me. I carefully return it to its resting place so that it may continue sleeping peacefully through the centuries. Unseen crickets and woodpeckers are loquacious guides along the trail, while hardy morning glories dress it up visually. Stately bunches of Harding grass, a European species, stand out among the more common oat grasses in the field.

If I turn around 180 degrees, I face the ranch house. I envision the two-story house set amongst an orchard (where the highway is now), the settler's children helping with chores, and the sounds and smells of horses, cows, geese, and chickens. The white siding on the house contrasts with the vivid blue sky background and the verdant green grass in the foreground. As mentioned before, John Melchisadek Grigsby and his brother Achilles constructed the middle section of the house in 1855. Additions that the Andersons made in 1885 to accommodate their six children included a parlor and bedroom downstairs, and two bedrooms upstairs.

Some of the original furniture remains in the ranch house for today's visitors to enjoy. There is a library table and a chest that belonged to the Anderson family. The piano in the ranch house, although quite old, did not belong to the Andersons. Handcrafted in a Chicago factory in 1919, the unique acquisition has a harpsichord pedal. The photograph hanging in the parlor depicts the original Anderson piano, which resides in the Lakeport Museum. Their piano, built in London, made the arduous journey to Lake County by way of a ship around Cape Horn, completing the trip by horse and wagon.

The original ranch house kitchen was razed and rebuilt in about 1918. It was equipped with electricity around 1924 when Lake County was powered. The windmill pump gave way to piped tap water. A modern bathroom was added at this time, off of the kitchen. The commode which sits in the bathroom sporting a chamber pot was the Andersons. The trusty chamber pot made a nighttime trek to one of the two outhouses unnecessary.

The ranch house looked out upon a hub of ranching activities. Everyone had a job- and there was plenty of work to go around. The branding corrals still stand. There were feed bins, mangers, milking troughs, pig pens, and other outbuildings which accommodated the livestock and facilitated the care of animals.

The fragments of clouds in the foothills above the marsh hold the promise of a spectacular sunset. Just before dusk the sky will become a watercolor canvas of opalescent coral colors. John Muir said, "Everybody needs beauty as well as bread, places to play in and pray in, where nature may heal and give strength to body and soul alike." I fix on the aerialist- a red-shouldered hawk winging over Anderson Marsh; a land of surprises and discovery. The rich complexity of this haven will continue to tell its story to all who will listen to the language of the land.

McVicar Trail

For a longer wander in Anderson Marsh take the McVicar Trail, a 3.5- mile trek running adjacent to the western boundary of the marsh. The McVicar Trail leads you through oak woodlands and grasslands, eventually leading you to a view across from Indian Island. One mild morning while walking with friends at Anderson Marsh along the McVicar trail we began to note a swarm of what we called 'ladybugs' flitting and flying along the trail with us. Later, we learned that insect geeks, or entomologists are using the name 'ladybird beetle' or 'lady beetle' since they are not true bugs. A bug, which is a type of insect, has a three-part body and belong to the order of insect called *Hemiptera*. It's amazing to know that these creatures belong to the almost 6,000-species ladybird beetle family, or *Coccinellidae*. I neglected to bring my hand-lens on the hike, but these may have been convergent ladybugs, the most common species in North America. In 2019 a cluster of ladybugs, known as a bloom or a loveliness, was so large it was spotted on the National Weather Service radar in southern California. This bloom was noted at 5,000 to 9,000 feet in the air. Since California is home to around 175 species of the insect it wasn't immediately clear which beetle species it was. When convergent lady beetles gather in a cloud like this in northern California, they typically mate and then migrate from the Sierra Nevada to various valleys below. They are not, however named for their behavior, but for the delicate white band near their head.

Lady beetles' life cycle is simple: eggs, larva, pupa, then, young lady beetle. An adult can lay ten to fifty eggs in a cluster each month, for one to three months. Their eggs are yellow and oblong. When the larvae emerge from the eggs, long and fierce-looking, they look nothing like lady beetles, but they commence to consuming thousands of aphids, mites, scale insects and mealy bugs. It takes several molts, or skin-shedding for them to reach the lovely little shape we know and enjoy.

These interesting little creatures hibernate over winter, often in aggregations, or groups when they hide in nooks and crannies like logs or hollow stems. In south Lake County, year after year in mid-June I have noted a bloom of lady beetles which arrive like magic, from the east and head west. If I stand with my arms outspread I am treated to a delightful polka-dot experience of little red essences that lovingly land on me before heading out on their lady beetle ways!

Gardeners understand that lady beetles, called ladybirds in many other parts of the world, are beneficial insects, as the majority of the species are, so they depend on these voracious beetles to consume aphids that can be detrimental to food and flower gardens. Many of our local garden shops stock lady beetles. Also, to encourage them to your garden plant flowers with pollen-rich blooms. They appear to take to the flat-topped flowers like marigold, yarrow, fennel and angelica which are also great companion plants that discourage 'bad bugs' in the garden.

Over the centuries people have been fascinated by lady

beetles. Some cultures consider them as good luck, while others have created nursery rhymes and poetry around the critters. It would be sad indeed to imagine a world without these glossy, red helpers that inhabit our forests and gardens while quietly going about their little lives.

Along with abundant living creatures like insects and secretive mammals like mountain lions and black-tailed deer at Anderson Marsh, a tremendous variety of duck species can be found here, many of which were once hunted by the Pomo people. Then, specialized throwing stones were utilized. To launch the mass-produced throwing stones with great force, specially made sling-shots were fashioned to hunt ducks in the marsh, creek and on Clear Lake. The round, golf-ball sized throwing stones were hardened in cooking fires prior to hunting waterfowl.

Included in the myriad species of waterfowl that thrive in and around Anderson Marsh are Western grebes, Clark's grebes, pied-billed grebes, geese, mergansers and more. American coots also find the lake and nearby surrounding waterways attractive. American coots may have been hunted for their plump protein. These duck-like birds are about the size of a chicken. American coots' tell-tale features include dark gray plumage and a white bill ringed with black. Coots are a relative of the rail, and are often viewed via their habits of diving and dining on plant-life harvested from the lake, and can also be seen hunting for tidbits along the shoreline. They feast on an assortment of worms, bugs and fish along with other bird's eggs. Coots rely on aquatic plants and stems to construct their floating nests which both sexes create together. Throughout their nesting season the males are commonly seen punting intruders with their lobed toes in order to defend their territory. Coots differ from ducks in that they do not possess webbed feet, but instead possess odd-looking oversized feet designed to aid in maneuvering muddy marshes and flats. When coots take wing they can be seen dashing across the waterways prior to lifting off. Coots have a habit of bobbing their heads while navigating the waters, making for some additional outdoor entertainment. Coots are hardy and can be viewed almost all over North America, particularly during winter months when they collect at marshes, ponds and lakes. Listen carefully to coot's croaks and grunts while bird-watching at the marsh.

The McVicar Trail takes you through dreamy cottonwoods. As their drifting fairy- like seeds float down I look up and note that some of the trees are criss-crossed with wild grapevines. Wild grape vines were sometimes utilized by Indigenous people when the vines were fashioned into sturdy, flexible cord. Then, the cord could be used for rims of baskets, such as cone-shaped carrying baskets. The hardy vines were gathered year round and stored for use at any time of the year. They could be soaked in water to soften them. Soaking with the addition of ashes was useful for bark-removal in order to split the vines into two strands and use for a type of thread. The vines were useful for lashing bundles as well. The fruit ripened in summer and was consumed dried, fresh or as a fruit or juice. Early Californians used wild grape leaves soaked in water as a poultice for wounds as well.

Along with the wild grape vines you may view Shannon Ridge Winery's vineyards climbing up the hillside to the left. Recently Lake County has become a popular destination not only for its natural beauty, agriculture and tourism, but for its dozens of award-winning wineries. It wasn't too long ago when there were only a mere handful of wineries in Lake County. Grape growers from the Napa Valley have long known about the rich volcanic soils and Mediterranean climate that make Lake County a fantastic choice for grapes of nearly all varietals to be grown here.

    My husband, Tom was partners in Lower Lake Winery, the first winery in Lake County since Prohibition. Lower Lake Winery was located south of Lower Lake on Highway 29. Groundbreaking occurred in 1976, with the first crush, Cabernet Sauvignon taking place in 1977. During its operation Lower Lake Winery garnered numerous awards for its fine wines. The Lake County Grape Growers Association pamphlet, and Wine Country Publication made note, in 1982, that this was the first winery in Lake County since Prohibition. It was also mentioned in renowned wine writer, Leon D. Adams' book, *The Wines of America*, third edition for that distinctive fact. He said, "When it opened in 1977, it was the county's first new winery to start since the Prohibition era. Alhambra orthopedic surgeon Dr. Harry Stuermer and his wife Marjorie financed the redwood building, its stainless-steel tanks and oak barrels, for their winemaker son Daniel, his wife Betty, Dan's sister Harriet, and her husband, Tom Scavone." In 1920 national Prohibition ended Lake County's early winemaking. That's when grapevines were replaced by walnut and pear orchards. In 1979 the winery was sold to Ployez Winery. Lower Lake Schoolhouse Museum displays Lower Lake Winery's original sign along with other winery related artifacts.

Across the marsh two graceful black-tailed deer graze. They spy me with their soft but intelligent eyes. This species resides along California's coast on up to Alaska, usually browsing blackberries, maple, grasses and more at the edge of a forest. Most active during the early mornings or dusk the beauties seem to vanish as if by magic.

There are many Pomo myths which involve deer, as the creatures were so important in their culture. Anthropologist Alfred Kroeber said, "The California Indians were in an animistic state of mind, in which they attributed life, intelligence, and especially supernatural power, to virtually all living and lifeless things." The Indigenous people of Lake County, including Pomo, Miwok, Yuki, Wappo, and Patwin all included mythology into their assorted cultures. Some Native groups were known to travel to acquaint others with the stories, or myths in order to explain their world views. Storytellers were sometimes presented with gifts of food, furs or baskets. In *Pomo Myths* S. A. Barrett says, "In fact this region was an ideal 'Indian country', and here there was developed a special culture, with certain variants in each of the environmental units. Such variations are reflected even in the mythology of the people."

Western traditional literary mythology has come to mean those stories which are imaginary, fantasy or fairy tales. Anthropological, historical, archaeological and other studies of mythology have come to appreciate and value the meaning of myth in Native American culture. Most California Indians were of the oral tradition, hence, the true connotation of myth is obscured by writing it down, and it loses a great deal in the language translation. Myths of many varieties were important to Indigenous people. Some of the subjects were cosmogonic, or origin myths- how the world came into being. Joseph

Campbell's works portray rich meaning in myths across the world. He has discovered themes that play out over and over across the cultures, such as the world coming into being from nothing (Mayan, Greek, Austrailian, First Book of Genesis), or that of materialization from the lower worlds such as that of the Hopi and Navajo.

Traditions of the past carry on. These traditions are important, when so many have faced obliteration. Paula Gunn Allen stated in *Spider Woman's Granddaughters- Traditional Tales and Contemporary Writing by Native American Women*, "Indian storytellers seldom write or speak as isolated individuals, cut off from their communal context. Rather, they use their tales to entertain, enlighten, educate, and above all to reveal to the audience their connection to the wisdom and experience of the tribal group. In this way the continuity between daily life and the tribal matrix is reaffirmed, and the audience's participation in the sacred life of the group and of the universe gains an added dimension."

Myth, it is currently understood, is of immeasurable magnitude to each culture's instruction. When the stories are no longer told then it serves to follow that they are no longer in your mind. With the loss of myth, perspective about what's occurring in a culture's day-to-day life is lost. This valuable information from ancient times has everything to do with ideas we have, our religion, problems we may face, and life passages. The stories and traditions become a rich source of meaning for life.

In the Pomo myth Coyote Transforms people into Animals, the people of the village had been rejoicing that they had the sun and it was set in its proper place where it could readily bestow light to all. They celebrated with blankets, baskets, food and beads to present to the crows for their part in hanging up the sun. It wasn't long before Coyote announced his displeasure that the people were not doing as he told them; but instead, he announced, that people did not appear to care about doing things the proper way. He scolded them by telling them that they may as well be animals and continue to do things the way they chose. Coyote then turned them all into animals and birds, saying, "You shall always live in the mountains. You shall be afraid and will be shot for meat. Your name shall be Deer. And so on he went naming each with an animal name and behavior to match.

As the marsh opens up to divulge Cache Creek, then Clear Lake, colorful crawdads scoot under the shores that are providing a meditative lapping soundtrack to the walk. A concerto of movement is always afoot merely for the price of showing up. From the grandeur of the oak-studded hillsides replete with ever-changing light and the continuous shows within the tree-canopy, to swirling patterns in the water's surface that can reveal a mink slinking by, a playful river otter or fish jumping for insects, the park draws me in. Anderson Marsh State Historic Park continually allows me to take a gleaming and touching odyssey across the landscape with each walk; and allows my heart and mind to dream.

Cows in the Marsh

John Still Anderson and his wife, Sarah

Andersons 1889: Standing L to R: Mora, Willie, Agnes
Seated L to R: Russell, John Still, Sarah, Grace and Charlie

L to R Archaeologist John Parker and California State Park's Archaeologist Breck Parkman

Anderson Ranch House 1880s

Ranch House today

Big Head Dance, Elem Tribe, Anderson Marsh, 1987

Dr. John Parker and wife, Cheyanne at the Emmy Award ceremony in San Francisco, June of 2017. "A Walk Through Time: The Story of Anderson Marsh" won in the "Historic/Cultural-Program/ Special" category in the 46th annual Northern California Emmy Awards.

Western grebe
Photo by Kathleen Scavone

Muskrat, some of the prolific wildlife in the park

Egret
Photo by Kathleen Scavone

Rock Art Anderson Marsh

Cupules in rock

Photo Credit courtesy of Dr. John Parker, and Breck Parkman

"A WALK THROUGH TIME"
AWARD-WINNING DOCUMENTARY ABOUT ANDERSON MARSH

Available on PBS online at:

https://www.pbs.org/video/kvie-viewfinder-walk-through-time/

The documentary, "A Walk Through Time" has garnered both the Governor's Historic Preservation Award in Sacramento in 2015, as well as an Emmy Award in the category of "Historic/Cultural-Program/Special" at the 46th annual Northern California Emmy Awards ceremony in San Francisco. Those present to collect the Emmy Award were the film's production team members Director Dan Bruns of the Advanced Laboratory for Visual Anthropology at California State University, Chico; archaeologist Dr. John Parker, another of the producers, along with his wife, Cheyanne, who also is an archaeologist; Executive Producer Leslie Steidl, a retired associate state archaeologist with the California Department of Parks and Recreations; and Eduardo Guaracha, the superintendent of the California State

Parks Northern Buttes District, which includes Lake County".

The film describes the significance of Anderson Marsh State Historic Park, as well as the formation of the park. The 28 minute film made its world premier in Clear Lake, California during the summer of 2015. Then, actor Peter Coyote was on hand to introduce the documentary to the public. The documentary is the result of the efforts of the local Koi Indian Tribe, California State Parks, Anderson Marsh Interpretive Association, archaeologists Dr. John Parker and Greg White, geoarchaeologist Jack Meyer, retired State Parks Ranger Tom Nixon, Koi Nation Chair Darin Beltran and Vice Chair Drake Beltran. The abundantly informative film gives an outline of our local gem, Anderson Marsh State Historic Park, while incorporating interviews with key players in the birth of the park, spectacular cinematography and exceptional narration by Dino Beltran. The concentrated efforts to preserve the land that is now Anderson Marsh State Historic Park began with Parker's hard work, along with many, many local supporters, culminating in the creation of the 1,300 acre park in 1982. The documentary addresses Anderson Marsh's wetlands, oak woodlands and grasslands. It tells of the park's cultural aspects which includes dozens of Native American archaeological sites that are situated in the park, some of which are over 14,000 years old.

The film, along with a related curriculum which I authored, were released to all Lake County elementary schools by Raeann Bossarte, State Park Interpreter 1, Northern Buttes District and recently retired State Parks Archaeologist, Leslie Steidl,. The expectations are that teachers in grades 3-5 will utilize the teaching resources in their classrooms in order to educate students on this unique and important site.

THE MAKING OF A STATE PARK
by Dr. John Parker

John Parker recounts the steps taken to preserve the valuable land that is now Anderson Marsh State Historic Park.

During the summer of 1976, John Parker, a student at Sonoma State University, moved to Lake County. The county wasn't new to him; he had been spending Easter week and a portion of every summer in the county since he was about 8 years old. When he was a freshman at Sonoma State in 1971, he conducted his first archeological survey in the area. He spent his last semester commuting from Lake County to Cotati in order to attend classes.

That summer, in 1976, the State Attorney Generals Office entered into a contract with Sonoma State to have the land around Anderson Marsh inspected so that any archeological sites in the area would be recorded. Parker, in order to obtain information for a class project, had already contacted the owner of the Anderson Ranch and Marsh and obtained permission to look over the area. It was only logical that he got the job as field director for the Anderson Marsh survey. The survey was conducted with a crew of five Sonoma State students and one Lake County resident.

Parker and his crew of archeologists couldn't believe what they encountered. Virtually everywhere they looked they found evidence of ancient Indian life. Some of the sites were the remains of Indian villages where up to 200 or 400 people once lived; some were smaller seasonal campsites; and some areas were used for special purposes such as stone tool manufacturing areas, and food collecting sites. No one on the crew had seen such a high concentration of archeological sites before. There was an average of one site for every 15 to 20 acres of land.

Finishing his Bachelors Degree in anthropology/archaeology, Parker got a temporary job as an archeologist with Caltrans in Sacramento. While in the capitol city he got to know other archeologists in the State Office of Historic Preservation. Realizing that land development would ultimately destroy the sites in the Anderson Marsh area, he started looking for ways to protect these cultural resources. With the help of the people in the Office of Historic Preservation and about 6 months of his spare time, Parker completed the forms necessary to nominate the newly recorded sites to the National Register of Historic Places.

In 1977, after review on both the state and federal levels, the Anderson Marsh Archeological District was added to the National Register of Historic Places. Parker breathed a sigh of relief because the listing on the Register indicated that the sites were significant and should be considered before development permits were issued in the area. He felt that the National Resister Listing would protect the sites.

Parker shifted his activities to giving slide shows and talks to civic clubs and citizen groups around Lake County. He conducted workshops on archeology for county school teachers to help provide innovative ways to teach the basics in school. His main interest was in increasing the public's awareness of the archeology resources which Lake County possessed.

Within one year after its inclusion on the National Register, 3 sites within the Anderson Marsh Archeological District had been destroyed. One three acre Indian village had a county sewer line put right through the middle of it. Three human burials were exposed in the walls of the sewer trench. It had become obvious to Parker that the National Register listing alone wouldn't preserve the resources. He began exploring other ways to protect the sites.

Parker began working on a scheme to buy one of the islands in the marsh area which had been listed for sale. The island had been abandoned for many years and would make an ideal location for an archeological research center. From there he could work on protecting the rest of the sites in the Archaeological District. The State Office of Historic Preservation could make matching funds available to help in the purchase. Parker contacted Helen Dodd, the owner, and made two offers for the island. The offers were referred to Mrs. Dodd's accountant who decided against them. Two months later, Helen Dodd died and the island went to a new owner through the will.

Striking out with that idea, Parker decided, "Why not go for the whole Archaeological District?" By giving his public talks and slide shows, he had gotten to know many people in the county and through them was able to make contact with both the Nature Conservancy and the National Audubon Society. Parker went to both of these groups in an attempt to persuade them to purchase the area as a preserve. But no luck.

In 1979, the State Department of Parks and Recreation started advertising for public input for projects to be funded by a proposed bond act which was scheduled to go before the California voters in 1980. Proposition 1, the State Park Bond Act was designed to provide over 300 million dollars for the acquisition and development of parks. After three weeks of weighing the positive and negative sides to having the area turned into a state park, Parker went to the Office of Historic Preservation to find out more about the State Park system. His friends within the system indicated that the parks department had a new classification for State Parks which offered protection to sensitive resources such as archaeological sites. These were called "Cultural Preserve State Parks." That is what Parker needed to hear. He made his decision.

In 1980 Parker entered graduate school at U.C. Davis. He also started on a campaign to get public support for the new state park. He presented the idea to civic clubs, citizen groups, the Lake County Supervisors, Native American Communities, the Department of Fish and Game, the County Chamber of Commerce, and other organizations. Everyone was in full support. When he had obtained an initial wave of support, he developed a presentation, filled out the forms, and on April 30, 1980, nominated the area to the State Parks Commission for acquisition as a Cultural Preserve under the proposed bond act funds.

In his efforts to obtain the initial support, Parker learned about many other resources which the area contained. The Department of Fish and Game had studied the ecosystem of Clear Lake and had concluded that the Anderson Marsh area was essential to fish reproduction in the Lake. The local Audubon Society had made a list of birds and other wildlife found in the area, some of which were on National Rare and Endangered lists. Members of the Native American community who visited the area pointed out plant materials used for basket making, food, and medicine. The county Historical Society members told Parker about the significance of the Anderson Ranch house which was built on the property in the 1870s.

Hearing about the nomination of the area for a new state park, landowners in the area had several different reactions: Some were opposed to the idea, some thought it a good idea as long as they got fair market value for their property, some decided to take steps to increase the fair market value of the property by applying for development permits, and one individual took a bold step and donated 240 acres of his Land to the National Audubon Society as a preserve.

Parker worried about those who had applied for development permits. This meant that it would be a race between his ability to obtain the acquisition funding and their ability to obtain the necessary permits for development.

With the help of Chamber of Commerce director, Ed Rogers, Parker pulled out all the stops. He set up and conducted boat tours of the area for State Park personnel, Fish and Game representatives, National Park Service people (in case the state acquisition fell through), senatorial and assembly aids, Corps of Engineers representatives, attorneys from the State Attorney General's Office, State Lands Commission personnel, County Public Works and Planning representatives, and many others.

After two aborted attempts at flying into Lake County during bad weather, the Channel 3 News Team from Sacramento finally made it up in their helicopter and did a nice five minute news spot about the proposed park area. The local Clearlake newspaper, The Clear Lake Observer, took a personal interest in promoting the park acquisition by covering new developments in the acquisition attempt and, when necessary, urging people to write letters of support.

The developers were moving fast also. One landowner applied for planning and Corps of Engineers permits to allow a 250 space mobile home park on a piece of land immediately adjacent to the marsh. Luckily for park supporters, this permit was denied. Another landowner was looking for an engineer to help put together plans for a large residential community. Seeing the problems that the previous developer encountered with the Corps of Engineers, this land owner offered to construct a Proposed Corps project in the area in exchange for the necessary permits.

Proposition 1 passed, so the Department of Parks and Recreation was busily ranking projects in order of importance. Unfortunately, Anderson Marsh was far down the list and it appeared that acquisition may not occur for ten years. Fearing that he wouldn't be able to hold off the developers that long, Parker made a trip to Sacramento and met with Doug Bosco, Assemblyman for Lake County. Those of you who believe in divine intervention, luck, karma, or whatever other name is given to supernatural action will not be surprised by what took place. Parker was amazed and has since become a believer in good karma.

Having very little knowledge of the political workings of State government, Parker's meeting with Doug Bosco was a shot in the dark. At best, he had hoped to persuade Bosco to author a bill to provide funds for the park. At worst, he expected to end up back at square one. Parker explained the position of the Anderson Marsh project on the Park Acquisition list and outlined the problem of local investors trying to obtain development permits.

Assemblyman Bosco picked up the phone and called the Park Director's Office and suggested that they advance the

Anderson Marsh project upward on their acquisition list.

Unknown to Parker at the time was the fact that Bosco was the Chairman of the Assembly Resources and Transportation Committee. This committee had the job of reviewing and voting on the State Parks Department budget. Parker's meeting with Bosco came just before the budget review, so, not wanting to cross a prominent player in their budget process, the State Park Director instructed his planning staff to initiate real estate assessments and other processes necessary to move the project forward.

It was a simple case of being in the right place at the right time and talking to the best person possible. It was total luck, karma, or possibly supernatural intervention.

In 1981, two million dollars was appropriated from the Energy Resource Fund to acquire the Anderson Marsh State Park. Also in 1981 John Parker received his Master's Degree in anthropology/archaeology from the University of California, Davis. Unfortunately, also in 1981, the State of California went into debt. In an effort to control state spending, Governor Brown froze several funding sources, including the Energy Resource Fund. These funds were never allocated to the Anderson Marsh project and were eventually diverted into the State general fund to help offset the budget deficit.

On the development front, a change of County Supervisors created a change in the political climate of Lake County. The change was toward pro-development. One of the Anderson Marsh landowners applied for annexation into the local sewer district which would have paved the way for residential development and increased the cost of the land to the State. Fortunately, Parker had obtained enough local support that the sheer number of people who turned out at the Supervisor's

Meeting caused the development-oriented board to vote against the annexation. But two weeks later, at the request of the owner/developer, the Board changed its mind without a public hearing.

In addition, several land use designations were changed by the Board of Supervisors in response to owner/developer requests. One such change turned the "intensive agricultural" designation of the land comprising Anderson Marsh into "suburban residential" and "suburban reserve" land. This created another increase in land value.

Preparing for the 1982 state budget hearings, the Parks and Recreation Planning Staff re-evaluated the real estate assessment of the Anderson Marsh Park area and upped their funding request to $3,118,000.00.

Parker initiated another all out effort to generate public support for the park project. This time letters were needed to persuade the Assemblymen and Senators to vote in favor of the project. In addition, letters to the Governor were needed to make sure the funds wouldn't be frozen again. Meanwhile, the owner of Anderson Marsh applied for a General Plan Land Use Amendment which would allow over one thousand homes to be built in the archaeologically sensitive area immediately adjacent to Anderson Marsh.

Parker made another round of presentations and slide shows of the area. He was able to obtain resolutions of support from the Clearlake City Council and the Conference of California Historical Societies. A change in the internal make-up of the Lake County Chamber of Commerce, causing a shift from promoting tourism to one of promoting industrial development prevented the Chamber from passing a resolution supporting the Park.

With the financial aid of the local Redbud Audubon Society, Parker developed flyers and posters which urged people to write to their Legislators. During the spring and early summer of 1982 Parker spent weekends rowing his boat around Anderson Marsh and Cache Creek handing out flyers to fishermen and picnickers in the area. The local resorts passed out flyers to their visitors and displayed posters supporting the State Park acquisition.

Parker made several trips to the state capitol to monitor the progress of the funding for the state park. He contacted the two new legislators who were to represent Lake County and brought them up to speed on the park project. The Senate Subcommittee voted in favor of the $3,118,000.00 appropriation for the Anderson Marsh.

On July 13, 1982 the Assembly Subcommittee on Resources and Transportation was to meet to go over the Parks and Recreation budget. It was the last day of months of State budget hearings and all the legislators were weary of the weeks of arguing about state expenses.

The hearing started at 7:00 a.m. Parker left Lake County at 5:00 a.m. to be there. The Anderson Marsh appropriation was put off as other legislators circulated in and out of the subcommittee meeting all day promoting their own personal projects. It appeared that Committee Chairman Doug Bosco was ignoring the Anderson Marsh project deliberately. The day dragged on . . .12:00 lunch . . .3:00 break…6:00 everyone was tired and hungry.

With just a few things left on the agenda (all of which had been passed by the Senate side of the legislature), Doug Bosco suggested that the subcommittee pass the rest as per the recommendation of the Senate. The vote was unanimous. Anderson

Marsh was one of those few things left on the agenda.

The meeting finally broke up at 7:00 p.m. and Parker walked over to Park Director Pete Dangermond who smiled and said, "Well, you got the money for Anderson Marsh." Parker responded by saying, "Yes, but it's a long way between appropriation and allocation, as we saw last year."

Later, in a conversation with assemblyman Bosco, Parker learned that he had deliberately put off talking about the Anderson Marsh funds. He had done this because of the fact that one of the committee members had expressed some disagreement about the funding of the park. Bosco was waiting, hoping that this committee member would leave the room momentarily so he could bring up the Anderson Marsh appropriation,

Meanwhile, the County had set July 29, 1982 as the date for the public hearing on the Anderson Ranch general plan land use amendment to allow over 1,000 new homes on the property. The Lake County Planning staff sent out packets to appropriate agencies for review and comment. The hearing date was listed in the local newspaper. Parker called all of the agencies which had received the packets to make sure that as many as possible responded. Parker's parents, Weldon and Dee, had circulated a petition through their neighborhood (directly across Cache Creek from Anderson Marsh) opposing the land use change. One week before the public hearing, John Parker went on a local radio talk show and spoke about the park and the upcoming public hearing.

Six years of work to protect a freshwater marsh and over fifty prehistoric Indian sites was coming down to a last stand. If the land use amendment passed, then the $3,118,000.00 would not be enough to buy the property. The decision was out of Parker's hands and was now in the hands of the people of Lake County. If the residents of Lake County wanted a new state park, they would have to show up at the public hearing and voice their concerns.

Parker walked through the Courthouse doors, briefcase in hand, and headed for the Supervisor's Chambers. When he entered the room, he was greeted by the eyes of over 95 people. The room was packed. Members of virtually every civic club in Lake County were there. The president of the Farm Bureau, representatives from the Department of Fish and Game, State Lands Division, the Native American community, and the Audubon Society all supported the park acquisition.

Choosing not to attend the meeting, the owner/developer asked for an extension by phone. The Planning Commission could not legally grant an extension, and so the owner/developer withdrew his land use change request.

Eight weeks later the Department of Parks and Recreation finalized negotiations with the major land owner and purchased 700 acres of the proposed 900 acre park.

Parker's dream for 6 years had become a reality.

Anderson Marsh Chronology

10-14,000 Years Ago - The first people entered the Clear Lake basin from the east.

6,000 Years Ago - The Clear Lake shore is populated and utilized.

4,500 Years Ago - The population of lake people expands to the surrounding areas of Napa and Russian River area.

4,000 Years Ago - The Lakeshore people began using upland resources, population is increasing.

3,000 Years Ago - Acorn processing came into use, a population decline occurred, shell bead money economy began, and social organization occurred.

2,000 Years Ago - A major population increase occurred, and bow and arrow in use.

1811 - Russian fur trappers from Fort Ross visit Clear Lake.

1820s - Euro-American hunters and Hudson Bay Trappers explored Lake County.

1841 - Salvador Vallejo had a Southeastern Pomo village massacred.

1850 - Bloody Island Massacre under command of Captain Lyon occurred.

1861 - The County of Lake was formed. Prior to this, the area was part of Napa County's "Hot Springs Township."

1867 - Father Osuna founded Mission St. Turibius three miles north of Kelseyville.

1855-70 - Achilles Fine and John Melchisadeck Grigsby homesteaded here. The central section of the ranch house was built.

1866-68 - Winter floods devastated many ranches around the lake, including the Grigsby's due to the dam which Clear Lake Water Works Co. built on Cache Creek. The Grigsbys won a lawsuit, then an appeal to the Supreme Court reversed the decision on legal technicalities.

1870 - Grigsby sold the ranch to the Clear Lake Water Works Co.

1870-82 - Clear Lake Water Works Co. transferred title to its subsidiary corporation, California Agriculture Improvement Association.

1884 - Grigsby moved to Butte Falls, Oregon, returning to Lake County several years later. He was buried at Lower Lake Cemetery.

1885 - John Still Anderson, Scottish immigrant, bought the ranch and lived here with his wife, Sarah, and six children, raising cattle.

1886 - The Andersons added the tallest wing to the house.

1912 - John Still Anderson passed away. Four of his unmarried adult children ran the ranch, raising stock instead of dairy cows. His oldest son, John Russel, lived in a house just south of the ranch and continued to actively manage the ranch.

1914 - Clear Lake Dam built.

1918 - Original kitchen wing of ranch house torn down and replaced.

1920s-30s - Children of Agnes Anderson Haggitt, John Still's youngest daughter, lived and worked on the ranch. In 1923 electricity and plumbing modernized the house.

1920s - Native Americans continued to inhabit Slater and Indian Islands.

1950s - Native Americans still gathered to fish and trap mudhens on Clear Lake.

1960s - Members of the Anderson family continued to live on and work the ranch.

1960s - Raymond Lyons purchased the ranch.

1972 - Spring, John Parker recorded his first archaeological site at Anderson Marsh for a class at Sonoma State University.

1978 - Anderson Marsh officially classified as an Archaeological District and listed on the National Register of Historic Places.

1982 - The State of California, realizing the archaeological significance of the marsh, acquired the ranch property. This event occurred due to John Parker's unflagging efforts along with community efforts.

1983 - October 15, Dedication ceremonies for Anderson Marsh

Park were held at the Anderson Ranch House with about 3,000 in attendance.

1985 - June 14, State Park commission officially names and classifies the Anderson Marsh project as the Anderson Marsh State Historic Park.

1991 - The park encompassed 941 acres, with the addition of Garner Island.

1999 - The park encompassed 1,065 acres.

Bibliography

Allen, Elsie
 1972 *Pomo Basket Making,* Naturegraph Publishers, Happy Camp, CA.

Bancroft, Hubert Howe
 1886 *History of California Vols. I-V11,*The History Company Publishers, San Francisco.

Barrett, S.A.
 1933 *Pomo Myths,* Cannon Printing Co., Milwaukee, WI.

Brown, Vinson and Douglas Andrews
 1990 *The Pomo Indians of California and Their Neighbors,* Naturegraph Publishers, Happy Camp, CA.

Department of Parks and Recreation
 1992 *California State Parks Docent Manual*

Gifford, Edward W. and Gwendoline Harris Block
 1990 *California Indian Nights,* University of Nebraska Press, Lincoln and London.

Goodrich, Jennie and Claudia Lawson, Vana Parrish Lawson
 1980 *Kashaya Pomo Plants,* Heyday Books, Berkeley, CA.

Harper and Row
 1981 *Complete Field Guide to North American Wildlife-Western Edition*

Heizer, R.F. and M.A. Whipple
1971 The California Indians- A Source Book, University of CA Press, Berkeley.

Heizer, Robert F. & Alan F Almquist
1971 The Other Californians- Prejudice and Discrimination under Spain, Mexico, and the United States to 1920, University of California Press, Berkeley, CA.

Hubbell, Sue
1993 Broadsides from the Other Orders- A Book of Bugs, Random House, New York.

Kirov, George
1994 William B. Ide- The President of California, Pub. by the Senate of the State of California.

Kroeber, A.L.
1925 Handbook of the Indians of California, Dover Pub., Inc. New York.

Menefee, C.A.
1873 Historical and Descriptive Sketchbook of Napa, Sonoma, Lake, and Mendocino, James D. Stevenson, Ph. D., Fairfield, CA.

Microsoft
1995 Encarta - The Complete Interactive Multimedia Encyclopedia.

Moratto, Michael J.
1984 California Archaeology, Harcourt Brace, New York, NY.

National Audubon Society Field Guide to North American Trees
1980, Alfred A. Knopf, New York.

Parsons, Mary Elizabeth
1966 The Wild Flowers of California, Dover Publications, Inc., New York.

Pavlik, Bruce M. et al.
1992 Oaks of California, Cachuma Press and the California Oak Foundation.

Parker, Dr. John
1994 Dots on a Map: Using Cultural Resource Management Data to Reconstruct Prehistoric Settlement Patterns in the Clear Lake Basin, California UMI Dissertation Services.

Parker, Dr. John
Lake County Archaeology website:
http://wolfcreekarcheology.com/

Patterson, Dr. Victoria
1990 The Singing Feather - Tribal Remembrances from Round Valley, Mendocino County Library, CA.

Reilly, Edgar M. Jr.
1968 The Audubon Illustrated Handbook of American Birds, McGraw-Hill Book Company, New York.

Sarris, Dr. Greg
1993 Keeping Slug Woman Alive - A Holistic Approach to American Indian Texts, University of California Press, Berkeley, CA.

Sarris, Dr. Greg
1994 Mabel McKay- Weaving the Dream, University of California Press, Berkeley, CA.

Slocum, Bowen, and Bowen Publishers
1881 History of Napa and Lake Counties, California, San Francisco, CA.

Smithsonian Institution
1978 Handbook of North American Indians Vol. 8.

About the Author

Kathleen Scavone, M.A., is an educator, potter, poet and photographer. She was selected "Lake County Teacher of the Year by the Lake County Office of Education, and was chosen as one of ten state finalists in the "California State Teacher of the Year Awards" by the California Department of Education.

She is a freelance writer for The Press Democrat, Napa Valley Register, News From Native California, etc. She is the author of *People of the Water – a novella of the events leading to the Bloody Island Massacre of 1850*, and has also written curriculum for the Emmy Award-winning documentary, *A Walk Through Time-the story of Anderson Marsh*.

www.ingramcontent.com/pod-product-compliance
Lightning Source LLC
Chambersburg PA
CBHW072049290426
44110CB00014B/1608